OWEN HOPKINS

Architectural Styles

A Visual Guide

Published in 2014
by Laurence King Publishing Ltd
361–373 City Road
London EC1V 1LR
tel +44 20 7841 6900
fax +44 20 7841 6910
e-mail enquiries@laurenceking.com
www.laurenceking.com

A catalogue record for this book is available
from the British Library.

ISBN 978 178067 163 5

Designed by Rose-Innes Associates

Printed in China

FRONT COVER

Top Herzog & de Meuron, National Stadium
('Bird's Nest'), Beijing, China, 2003–08
(see Expressive Rationalism, page 213)

Bottom Choir, Gloucester Cathedral,
Gloucestershire, England, 1331–55
(see Late Gothic, page 37)

BACK COVER

Top left Richard Rogers and Renzo Piano,
Centre Georges Pompidou, Paris, France,
1977 (see High-Tech, page 192)

Top right Pont du Gard, near Nîmes, France,
ca. first century CE (see Ancient Roman,
page 13)

Bottom left Oscar Niemeyer, Plaza of
the Three Powers, Brasília, Brazil, 1958
(see Regionalism, page 197)

Bottom right Giacomo Leoni, Clandon Park,
Surrey, England, 1730–33 (see Palladianism,
page 101)

Contents

Introduction

The very notion of architectural 'style' is largely a creation of the nineteenth century, and, indeed, of the discipline of architectural history itself. The figure with whom the concept of 'style' is mostly closely associated during this period was the Swiss architectural historian Heinrich Wölfflin. A student of the influential German cultural historian Jacob Burkhardt, Wölfflin established an almost scientifically rigorous method for architectural history in charting what he described as the 'problem of the development of style'. He established five pairs of opposing concepts: linear/painterly; plane/recession; closed form/open form; multiplicity/unity; and absolute clarity/relative clarity. Armed with this framework, any architectural historian with the necessary visual education would be able to ascertain the 'style' of a particular work of architecture and chart its progression over time.

Wölfflin's method was criticized from different quarters. Some took issue with the way in which his apparent reduction of the experience of a work of art or architecture to a discrete set of parameters negated a subjective, intuitive or emotional response. Moreover, his theory tended to overlook content in favour of form, while ignoring the social, economic or material factors that determined the creation of a building or a work of art. In Wölfflin's essentially Hegelian conception, 'style' had its own life and its own trajectory, with artists and architects relegated to mere actors performing from a script pre-ordained by the zeitgeist. In some ways these criticisms tended towards a caricature of Wölfflin's theory and method. Nevertheless, they have decisively shaped attitudes to 'style', especially among historians taking a social-historical perspective, for whom 'style' is often perceived as determinist and elitist.

Thus in conceiving a book such as this, one is met with both conceptual and practical difficulties, not to mention historical ones; only since the nineteenth century have architects considered themselves proponents of one 'style' or another, no matter how one conceives it. Moreover, when drawing together works of architecture that exhibit certain shared 'stylistic' characteristics one is necessarily excluding others that do not. Shaped by individual minds and hands as much as broad trends, architecture of all periods demonstrates more variety than any 'stylistic' category could hope contain. 'Style' is therefore considered here in a broad sense; in some instances the term is used to group and analyze buildings according to very particular traits, and in others to highlight cultural trends or particular architectural strategies that bring together works that superficially might appear unrelated. Even in cases when architects came together to define their own movements, if not 'styles', in the twentieth century especially, one has to be highly aware of particular motives behind such associations. Individual architects' work does not necessarily remain consistent over their career; they may begin their career working in one 'style' and end it in quite another, and there are, of course, the architects whose work evades categorization altogether.

The book's nine chapters generally follow established periods or bodies of architecture. Within them each individual 'style' is conceived according to shared formal characteristics, geography, broad cultural trends, movements or ideologies – or any combination thereof. The focus is predominantly visual; while each 'style' receives a short introduction, six key characteristics are identified through captioned photographs. These range from the use of a distinctive window type or decorative moulding to materials or the particular ideas underlying the conception of a 'style'. In this way the book acts as both a reference point and something that is more instructive. While the notion of 'style' can be restrictive or exclusive, through its inherent processes of association and grouping, it has the power to uncover and elevate the overlooked.

Classical

Since the advent of the Classical Age in Athens, in the fifth century BCE, the classical language has been deeply woven into Western understandings of architecture and, indeed, of civilization itself. Its fundamental principle of imbuing architectural forms with the proportions and vitality of human ones has had lasting significance. However, despite the universal aspirations sometimes claimed for it, classical architecture was born from a very particular set of conditions and circumstances.

Origins

Several important Egyptian monuments, such as the Mortuary Temple of Queen Hatshepsut at Deïr-el-Bahari (mid fifteenth century BCE) and the Amun Temple at Karnak (1530–323 BCE), had made use of essentially columnar systems. However, the Minoan civilization on the island of Crete, which maintained links with Egypt, has increasingly been seen as important for developments on mainland Greece. Minoan architectural survivals, either excavated or in ruins, are mainly palace complexes in which can be seen the beginnings of the trabeation that defined classical architecture centuries later. While not unsophisticated, especially in their water management systems, the Minoans were little interested in architectural articulation, instead devoting most attention to wall paintings. However, the Mycenaean civilization (ca. 1600–1100 BCE), whose prominence coincided with the period illustrated in Homer's epics *The Iliad* and *The Odyssey*, began, primitively at first, to integrate decoration and structure in a way that prefigured classical architecture. An interesting example is the Lion Gate in Mycenae (ca. 1250 BCE): two jambs support a rectangular lintel, above which sits an ornamented triangular stone that in some ways can be seen as a primitive pediment.

The Orders

Classical architecture, which emerged in ancient Greece in the seventh century BCE, in the form of the first Doric temples, forged the columnar and trabeated systems into a coherent language of architecture in which the orders were the defining components. While at a practical level the orders were clearly load-bearing, their proportional rules and symbolic allusions – the Doric represented a man; the Ionic, a matronly woman; the Corinthian, the figure of a young girl – governed the composition of whole temples.

The triglyph and metope forms of the Doric order alluded to its earlier timber incarnations, and in early temples the Doric is more rudimentary and massive. It reached its apogee in the Parthenon, Athens (447–438 BCE), the greatest emblem of Greek architecture, which has drawn admirers including the nineteenth-century writer and poet Lord Byron and the Modernist architect Le Corbusier. The Parthenon was soon joined on the Acropolis by the Ionic Temple of Athena Nike (427–424 BCE) and the Erechtheion (421–405 BCE). The Corinthian order was usually reserved for interiors until the Hellenistic period which began after the death of Alexander the Great in 323 BCE. Historically associated with the decline of Greek civilization, and freer, lighter and more sculptural, Hellenistic culture gave rise to some of the greatest accomplishments of antiquity, among them the early-second-century Great Altar of Zeus at Pergamon, in present-day Turkey. The Altar is now partially reconstructed at the Pergamon Museum in Berlin.

Roman Innovation

The Hellenistic period continued until the advent of the Roman Empire with the reign of Augustus as the first emperor from 27 BCE to 14 CE. Roman art and architecture were heavily dependent on Hellenistic precedents, but developed to reflect quite different circumstances, as well as the requirements of managing and administering a huge empire. The fundamental divergences were the move away from Greek and Hellenistic architecture's reliance on columns, and the emergence of structural and material innovations – the arch, vault and later dome; and new types of brick and concrete – that facilitated the creation of some of antiquity's most enduring monuments, physically and conceptually.

Ancient Greek

Ancient Roman

Region: Greece and its Mediterranean colonies
Period: Seventh century to first century BCE
Characteristics: Trabeated system; Orders; Peristasis; Isolated temple; Proportion; Sculpture

The Parthenon in Athens represents the apotheosis of what is generally identified as the Classical Age, the period during the fifth and fourth centuries BCE in which culture, learning and democratic politics coalesced to inaugurate Western civilization. Under the direction of the great statesman and military commander Pericles, the architects Ictinus and Callicrates and the sculptor Phidias were charged with the creation of a new Parthenon, dedicated to the patron deity of Athens, Athena (the previous temple having been destroyed by the Persians, ca. 480 BCE). A huge three-stepped base was created on which was constructed a rectangular temple of seventeen columns on the north and south sides and eight on the east and west. Inside, the *cella* (the central room of a temple) contained a colossal golden statue of Athena by Phidias, now long lost.

Phidias also oversaw the creation of sculpture that was integrated into the building itself: pedimental groups depicted Athena's birth and her tussle with the god Poseidon; in the metopes were scenes of battles, between the gods and the giants, and between Greeks, Centaurs and Amazons; and the famous frieze, which ran around the top of the *cella*, showed a Panathenaic procession in honour of Athena. The naturalism of the Parthenon's sculpture, which is thought to have been painted in rich colours, stood in stark contrast to the stiff figures of the earlier Archaic period (ca. 700–480 BCE). Phidias's work marked a golden age of Greek culture. Sculptors such as Polyclitus, Praxiteles, Lysippos and Myron produced some of antiquity's greatest works of art (though now known only through Roman copies), while the tragedies of Aeschylus, Sophocles and Euripides similarly created new paradigms in the dramatic arts.

What gives the Parthenon the vitality of a work of architecture, as opposed to a geometrical experiment, are a number of subtle devices moulding its otherwise rigid order to human eyes. The ends of its base and entablature curve upwards slightly; the corner columns are slightly thicker than the others; and all its columns make use of entasis to mitigate the illusion of concavity created by an exactly parallel shaft. The geometric principles and human spirit inaugurated in the Parthenon would decisively shape Greek architecture as it moved from the Classical Age into the Hellenistic period.

Trabeated system

Composed from a series of vertical posts and horizontal transfer beams, ancient Greek architecture is at its root a trabeated system. Its key difference in that regard from Egyptian, Minoan or Mycenaean prototypes is its architectural articulation, which emerges as a symbolic language integrated with a building's proportional (and structural) logic.

Temple of Hera, Paestum, Italy, mid sixth century BCE

Orders

The most significant innovation of ancient Greek architecture and the principal components of a classical building, the orders are formed of a base, shaft, capital and entablature. Each of the Doric, Ionic and Corinthian orders has its own proportional system and symbolic attributes. The first two appeared in all periods of ancient Greek architecture, while the Corinthian became more prevalent during the Hellenistic period, notably in the Choragic Monument of Lysicrates.

Choragic Monument of Lysicrates, Athens, Greece, 334 BCE

Peristasis

Greek temples were designed according to a specific number of spatial and columnar arrangements. Most striking are the variations of peripteral temples that made use of peristasis: a single or double row of columns forming an external envelope and providing structural support. Peristasis is seen, for example, in the Temple of Zeus at the important Greek colony of Cyrene.

Temple of Zeus, Cyrene, Libya, fifth century BCE

Isolated temple

Constructed to house sacred cult statues of deities, Greek temples had interiors that consisted of variations of a discrete number of spatial configurations. People other than priests rarely entered temples, so these buildings were seen most often from afar. Their sites were carefully chosen and the temple was almost always oriented east–west.

Temple of Concordia, Agrigento, Sicily, fifth century BCE

Proportion

Ancient Greek architecture was governed by a strict proportional system that defined both plan and elevation, and the choice and size of the order employed determined all succeeding scales and ratios. Various optical refinements were used to reconcile the rigid geometry to the distorting effects of human vision, imbuing a building such as the Parthenon with energy and emotion.

Parthenon, Athens, 447–438 BCE

Sculpture

The classical language generally, and Greek temples specifically, provided much scope for sculptural ornamentation in metopes, friezes and pediments, and also for freestanding sculptures, either inside a temple or atop its pediment, called *acroteria*. The extraordinary 'Gigantomachy' frieze of the Pergamon Altar is one of the high points of Hellenistic sculpture, inextricably tied to its architectural setting.

Great Altar of Zeus, originally Pergamon (now in Berlin), mid second century BCE

Region: Europe, especially Italy; the Mediterranean, including North Africa; Asia Minor and the Middle East
Period: First century BCE to fourth century CE
Characteristics: Arch; Walls; Orders; Vaults and dome; Monumentality; New building types

The Romans were deeply influenced by all aspects of Hellenistic culture. In architecture they essentially adopted the classical language and adapted it to new situations and uses. In contrast to ancient Greek prototypes, which were usually sited so as to be seen from afar, most monumental Roman architecture is in more enclosed or urban areas. This perhaps played a part in the shift from the Greek preference for colonnades towards the frequent Roman use of applied columns and pilasters to articulate a wall. The Romans utilized the Doric, Ionic and Corinthian orders in a far freer manner than the Greeks had, creating their own version of the Doric and using the Corinthian far more frequently. They also added two further orders to the repertoire: the Tuscan, a simpler, more massive version of the Doric derived from Etruscan architecture; and the Composite, a combination of the volutes of the Ionic with the Corinthian's acanthus leaves.

Not only did the Romans adapt the existing classical language, but they also made use of novel forms, and developed new construction techniques and ways of employing materials. The arch had been a feature of Etruscan architecture,

yet the Romans made it their own, utilizing it as both a structural and a symbolic device. The arch allowed the creation of great bridges and aqueducts, which eased the transport of food and water, facilitating the unprecedented concentration of people in urban centres. At its height Rome was home to more than 1 million inhabitants, many of whom were housed in multi-storey blocks called *insulae*, the construction of which was made possible by the innovative use of the arch in brick and concrete.

The arch and other innovative construction methods enabled two further important developments: the vault and the dome. These were most frequently used in great bath complexes, such as those of Caracalla (ca. 215 CE) and Diocletian (ca. 306 CE) in Rome, and also in palaces, including Nero's first-century *Domus Aurea* (Golden House), Hadrian's early second-century villa at Tivoli and Diocletian's great palace at Spalato (ca. 300 CE), to which he retired after his abdication. Domes were also occasionally used in temples and the Pantheon (ca. 117–38 CE) in Rome remains both the greatest and the best-preserved example.

Arch

Able to span much wider distances than a simple trabeated system, the arch is arguably the defining feature of Roman architecture. The magnificent Pont du Gard, in southern France, used three levels of arches spanning a wide gorge to bring water to the Roman settlement at Nîmes. Arches were also erected to glorify emperors or commemorate military victories.

Pont du Gard, near Nîmes, France, ca. first century CE

Walls

While Greek temples frequently made use of peristasis, the Romans generally ascribed less importance to colonnades, particularly on side elevations. At the Maison Carrée, Nîmes, one of the best-preserved Roman temples, the columns behind the portico are engaged in a pseudoperipteral arrangement rather than freestanding as they might have been in a Greek temple.

Maison Carrée, Nîmes, ca. 16 BCE

Orders

The Romans adapted and augmented the Greek orders to reflect changing circumstances and new uses. As well as creating their own version of the Doric order, the Romans adapted the Ionic order so that – as seen in the Temple of Saturn – its volutes were angled, solving the problem of how to negotiate corners.

Vaults and dome

The arch provided the geometric basis for both the vault and the dome: the former was created by the extrusion of an arch along an axis, and the latter by rotating the arch 360 degrees through its centre. As well as having practical applications, the geometrical purity of both the vault and the dome – famously seen in the Pantheon, the temple to all the gods erected by the Emperor Hadrian (r. 117–38 CE) – had important symbolic connotations.

Temple of Saturn, Rome,
third or fourth century CE

Pantheon, Rome, ca. 117–38 CE

Monumentality

Architecture was highly important in representing the power and prestige of the Roman Empire in its colonized territories and also in Rome itself. Modelled on the earlier Arch of Septimius Severus, the Arch of Constantine commemorates the emperor's victory over Maxentius in 312 CE. Its eclectic sculptural adornments, including the use of spolia, reflect the fourth-century move away from the traditions of Hellenistic art and architecture.

Arch of Constantine, Rome, ca. 315 CE

New building types

The Romans created many new building types, such the forum, the hippodrome, the villa and the town house. They also created a new concept of the amphitheatre, the most famous example of which was the Amphitheatrum Flavium, Rome (known since medieval times as the Colosseum). It held various spectacles including gladiatorial combat. Its oval plan and the stacking of the orders on its exterior elevations had no precedents in Greek architecture.

Colosseum, Rome, ca. 75–82 CE

Early Christian

With the Edict of Milan of 313 CE the Roman emperor Constantine (r. 306–37) legalized Christian worship across the empire. Christianity was, of course, already more than 300 years old by this time, but due to their persecution Christians had worshipped in secret and their places of worship therefore remained hidden. Although Christianity was adopted as the official state religion of the Empire only after his reign, Constantine supported it through both political and legal reform and the building of a number of important churches, including St. Peter's Basilica on the site of St. Peter's burial in Rome. The temple form, with its overt pagan connotations, was, of course, out of the question as a model for buildings designed for Christian worship. The form of the basilica, a large colonnaded hall typically used for the conducting of business, was, on the other hand, well suited for adaption to Christian purposes, and it was this building type that formed the basis for many early churches, including St. Peter's.

Constantinople

At the time of the Edict of Milan, Constantine was emperor only of the western half of the empire, a position he had secured through his defeat of Maxentius in 312. The eastern half of the empire was under the rule of Licinius, with whom Constantine had co-issued the edict. The uneasy truce between the two did not last long and Constantine finally defeated Licinius in 324 to once again unify the Roman Empire. Shortly after, Constantine moved the imperial capital to the ancient Greek city of Byzantium, which he refounded as the new Rome. The city became known as Constantinople.

While the western part of the empire was soon overrun by invading Germanic hordes, the eastern half, though gradually diminishing in both scale and importance over the centuries, survived until its fall to the Ottoman Empire in 1453. From Constantine's initial and rapid building of its new capital, the Byzantine Empire evolved its own distinct art and architecture reflecting changing liturgical practices and theology. Largely emerging from Roman art, Byzantine art gradually diverged from the former's naturalistic basis to create images that bordered on the abstract. Painted in rich colours and decorated with gold or rendered in fine mosaic, Byzantine 'icons', which depicted Christ or other holy figures, became important objects for religious veneration. (However, they were also subject to systematic destruction, called iconoclasm, by those who believed they inspired idolatry.) Byzantine churches were similarly richly decorated with gold and mosaics, but the main difference between them and the earlier churches built by Constantine was undoubtedly the advent, from the sixth century, of the centralized space topped by often intersecting domes – a form that reached its apotheosis in the great church of Hagia Sophia.

Western Europe

The Great Schism of 1054 irrevocably separated what became known as the Roman Catholic and Orthodox Churches, yet well before, with the Western Empire largely overrun, architecture in the West had already taken its own path. Little in the way of consistent style can be inferred from the relatively few surviving works in Western Europe between the fifth and eighth centuries. What does survive indicates a loose continuation of the basilican plan and sporadic and somewhat primitive imitation of the classical orders. The main exceptions occurred during the reign of Charlemagne (r. 800–814), who was crowned Holy Roman Emperor in 800 by the Pope, the first for three centuries, and presided over a concerted revival of ancient learning and culture. The Palatine Chapel (consecrated in 805) is the only surviving component of his great palace at Aachen.

After Charlemagne's death his empire was soon fragmented, yet the social and economic foundations of the medieval period were already being laid, leading to the emergence during the eleventh century of the style known as Romanesque.

Byzantine

Romanesque

Region: Eastern Mediterranean
Period: Fourth to fifteenth century
Characteristics: Pendentive dome; Mosaics; Basilican; Centralized; Stylistic freedom; Brick and plaster

Constantine's choice of Byzantium as the site of the new imperial capital was largely due to its strategic position on the Bosphorus; it had a natural harbour and was well placed to repel Germanic tribes to the north and Persians to the east. Huge walls were erected around the city's perimeter and a ceremonial centre was laid out, with a forum, hippodrome, palace, senate and various monuments, including a great column (still surviving though relocated) topped by a statue of Constantine himself. He founded the great church of Hagia Irene, and the nearby church of Hagia Sophia was built soon after his death. Nothing of the original churches survives, although it can be assumed that they were of the basilican, typically early Christian, form that Constantine had built in Rome. The present domed structures date from the sixth century and, in the case of Hagia Sophia especially, represent the apotheosis of Byzantine architecture.

While the basilican churches were an adaption and continuation of a Roman building type, the domed Byzantine church was a notable development and departure from earlier forms. The Pantheon in Rome was, of course, the inescapable reference point for any domed space and Constantine's own Church of the Holy Sepulchre

in Jerusalem made use of a similarly centrally planned, though far smaller, dome arrangement. But the Byzantine dome was carried on pendentive arches, which had the important advantage of covering a square rather than a circular space. Moreover, in contrast to the basilican form, in which the central nave was defined by colonnades on either side, the domed Byzantine church had far greater expanses of wall surface that could be decorated with all manner of mosaics and other enrichments.

While the building is largely intact, Hagia Sophia's interior decoration was damaged during periods of iconoclasm and by the church's conversion into a mosque following Constantinople's fall to the Ottomans in 1453. The best surviving example of Byzantine architecture is the church of S. Vitale at Ravenna, Italy. It was built at about the same time as Hagia Sophia during the reign of Justinian I, who is depicted along with the Empress Theodora in its sumptuous mosaics. Although the Byzantine Empire would largely be driven out of Italy within two centuries, its influence remained, aided by ongoing trading links, especially with Venice where St. Mark's Basilica (begun ca. 1063) continued the Byzantine tradition.

Pendentive dome

Unlike the dome of the Pantheon, which rested on a circular base, the domes of Hagia Sophia and other Byzantine churches were supported by essentially square bases. To reconcile the different geometries, Byzantine domes sat on pendentives – curved triangular vaults that visually and structurally negotiated the gap between the four supporting round arches and the dome above.

Hagia Sophia, Istanbul, 532–7

Mosaics

The interiors of Byzantine churches were densely decorated with rich figurative and geometric mosaics. Those at the Basilica of S. Vitale are the most sumptuous to have survived. Various biblical scenes, all manner of flora and fauna, and figures of Jesus Christ and the Apostles are depicted in gleaming colours.

Basilica of S. Vitale, Ravenna, Italy, 527–48

Basilican

Ancient basilicas were essentially large halls, rectangular in plan with interior colonnades that created a central space surrounded by narrower aisles. Christian adaptions of the type, which informed Byzantine architecture, typically removed the end colonnades, inserted an apse at the east end for the altar, and sometimes added transept arms and a narthex at the west end.

Centralized

Early Christian churches were almost universally basilican in form. However, centralized plans, which were better suited to Byzantine liturgical practices, became increasingly prevalent. One of the most perfect is the Basilica of S. Vitale, which is not actually a basilica in the formal sense, but has curving columned screens mediating between a central octagon and a surrounding ambulatory.

Sta. Maria Maggiore, Rome,
432–40

Basilica of S. Vitale, Ravenna,
527–48

Stylistic freedom

Erected by Theodoric, King of the
Ostrogoths, as his palace chapel, the
Basilica of Sant'Apollinare Nuovo in
many ways represents a fusion between
the early Christian and the Byzantine
styles. While conforming to the basilican
type, its architectural articulation is
only loosely classical, with the inexact
imitation of an entablature supported
by characteristically Byzantine – and
unclassical – basket capitals.

Brick and plaster

Byzantine churches were typically
constructed of brick and plaster, often
visible as the exteriors were left
unadorned. Inside, the tesserae that
formed the mosaic decoration were
usually set on a bed of plaster on top
of the underlying brick structure. Having
been subject to iconoclasm, the bare
interior of Hagia Irene reveals how the
use of brick allowed the creation of its
complex geometrical structure.

Basilica of Sant'Apollinare Nuovo,
Ravenna, early sixth century

Hagia Irene, Istanbul, rebuilt
in the mid sixth century

Region: Europe
Period: Mid eleventh to mid twelfth century
Characteristics: West towers; Round arch; Apses; Barrel vault; Thick piers and columns; Severity

What fundamentally differentiates Romanesque – literally meaning 'resembling Roman' – from the architecture of the preceding period is its spatial organization. From the late tenth century a sense of spatial coherence and unity began to emerge through planning, for example in the second abbey at Cluny (consecrated in 981) and the slightly later church of St. Michael at Hildesheim. In contrast to the monotony of the basilican plan, a distinct rhythm is established in these churches through the repetitive spacing of piers and columns, which is punctuated by the crossing, a defining feature of the Romanesque.

The Normans were central to both the development and the spread of these new ideas. The key innovation in cathedral design, which the Normans introduced to England following their victory at the Battle of Hastings in 1066 and subsequent conquest, was the bay. Internal elevations were composed of stacked arcades of round arches resting on massive piers, which were tied together by subsidiary vertical shafts that served to define bays both as individual entities and part of a collective whole. Many early Romanesque cathedrals had flat ceilings, although tunnel vaults were also fairly common across Europe during the early twelfth century. Groin vaults had been invented by the Romans, but they were rarely used after the decline of the Roman Empire because of their geometrical complexity. However, the masons at Durham Cathedral in England felt confident enough to use them for the nave, prefiguring the Gothic (see page 26) in form, if not in structure. The applied ribs of the groin vault tie the opposing elevations together, creating a coherent spatial relationship.

The exteriors of early Christian and Byzantine churches were often left bare and unarticulated. In Romanesque architecture the exterior received far more attention. Increasingly, towers marked the intersection of the nave and the transept arms. However, the greatest exterior innovation is undoubtedly the twin-towered west front, seen, for example, in the Norman abbeys of La Trinité (begun ca. 1062) and St. Étienne (begun ca. 1067), both in Caen (though they are not the earliest examples).

Different regions created their own versions of Romanesque as the style spread across Europe, often via pilgrimage routes; the Romanesque cathedral at Santiago de Compostela in Spain was an important destination for pilgrims. With the advent of the Crusades at the end of the eleventh century, the increasing interchange of architectural ideas would see Romanesque soon make way for the Gothic.

West towers

The inclusion of twin towers in the west front of a cathedral or abbey was one of the great innovations of Romanesque architecture. Typically the towers flanked a central portal, which was often emphasized by the use of concentric arches and adorned with sculpture. Over time the single portal evolved into a tripartite portal.

St. Trinité, Caen, Normandy, France, begun ca. 1067

Round arch

Ancient Roman architecture made extensive and systematic use of the round arch, which was an essential element of some of its greatest achievements. Its use never died out during the intervening centuries, but it was only in Romanesque architecture that the possibilities of the round-arch arcade in both a structural and a spatial sense were once again exploited to the full.

Nave, Ely Cathedral, Cambridgeshire, twelfth century

Apses

The east end of an early Christian basilican church usually terminated with an apse – a semicircular recession in which the altar was placed. Apses are similarly a standard feature of Romanesque church architecture, appearing not only at the east end but also at the transept arms or even at the west end.

Barrel vault

While early Christian churches and cathedrals had timber roofs, barrel vaults were frequently used in Romanesque architecture. Formed by the extrusion of a single semicircular arch along an axis, barrel vaults require thick supporting walls. Thus they contribute indirectly to the apparent heaviness of the Romanesque in contrast to the Gothic.

Speyer Cathedral, Speyer,
Germany, 1024–61

St. Sernin, Toulouse, France,
begun ca. 1080

Thick piers and columns

Unlike the pointed arch of the later Gothic, the Romanesque round arch required the support of massive piers or columns. Monolithic piers were usually formed from an ashlar shell filled with rubble masonry. Columns were often composed of multiple shafts, which, as well as providing support, visually linked lower and upper arcade levels and helped define individual bays.

Severity

Romanesque architecture can be severe in its austere forms and geometric intensity, features that are especially characteristic of its Norman iterations. The cathedral of St. Front, originally an abbey, appears to be based on St. Mark's Basilica. Yet rather than being covered in mosaics, its pendentive domes are left unadorned, giving the interior an architectural force quite unlike that of its Venetian model.

Durham Cathedral, County Durham, England, 1093–1133

St. Front, Périgueux, France, early twelfth century

Gothic and Medieval

The birth of the Gothic in Europe can traced more or less to a new choir at the then abbey of Saint-Denis, near Paris, France, in 1140. Built under the direction of the revered Abbot Suger and consecrated in 1144, the choir (and its unknown designer) revolutionized architecture for at least the next 300 years. With the revival of the Gothic in the nineteenth century, its influence extended, indirectly, centuries further.

The features now considered integral to Gothic architecture – the pointed arch, the flying buttress and the rib vault – were in fact all employed in various ways in the preceding Romanesque style. One theory even holds that the origins of the pointed arch can be traced further back to early Islamic architecture. However, what was novel at Saint-Denis was the way in which these key features were employed together to create an integral and coherent whole. The pointed arch offered structural advantages that allowed cathedrals to be built higher, with oblong bays that were stronger than similarly sized square bays determined by the round arch of the Romanesque. The vaults were carried on ribs: projecting strips of masonry that supported the non-structural 'web' or infill. Flying buttresses – half-arch structures providing lateral support to a wall – helped carry the thrust of the nave's vault. Together these features gave Gothic cathedrals a dramatic verticality absent from the Romanesque. Moreover, the use of piers rather than thick walls as more efficient load-bearing elements enabled the interior spaces to be opened up, creating an overarching feeling of lightness – and making possible Gothic architecture's other great innovation: stained-glass windows.

Scholasticism

Gothic architecture reflected the prevailing tradition of Scholastic thought that dominated medieval theology and philosophy. Scholasticism, which arguably reached its apogee in Thomas Aquinas's *Summa Theologica* (1265–74), sought to blend the doctrines of the Church with ancient Greek and Roman philosophy. It held that truth was not something that could be discovered through reason or experiment, but already existed, pre-ordained by God. This lent great weight to the authority of the Church, which stood on the threshold between Heaven's perfection and the imperfect Earth, which had fallen from God's grace. In many ways the Gothic cathedral was intended to stand astride these two worlds. Often housing the relics of a saint or perhaps even a fragment of the Holy Cross, the cathedral offered a tangible link to the divine. This was echoed in the quasi-mystical complex geometry of its vaulting and, of course, in its sheer scale. The often sumptuous stained glass and sculpture of cathedrals had the dual function of relating the Christian story to a largely illiterate laity while also conveying a sense of the divine beauty of the Kingdom of Heaven.

International Gothic

The innovations of Saint-Denis quickly spread through the Île-de-France, with new cathedrals begun at such places as Noyon, Senlis, Laon and Chartres, and soon reached England. Masons and craftsmen carried the new style across borders. It was under the direction of one such craftsman, William of Sens, that the choir of Canterbury Cathedral, Kent, was begun in the new style in 1174.

From its beginnings in France and then England, Gothic architecture became prevalent in Germany, the Low Countries, Spain, Portugal and even Italy. It evolved over the succeeding centuries, being frequently remade and adapted – its use also extended beyond ecclesiastical architecture – before being superseded as the Renaissance swept across Europe. The legacy of Gothic architecture lived on, however, through both the cathedrals that populated the landscapes of many countries – centuries later still among the largest buildings around – and the imprint it had left on national and religious identities, which was brought to the fore in the nineteenth-century Gothic Revival.

Early Gothic

High Gothic

Late Gothic

Venetian Gothic

Secular Gothic

Castle

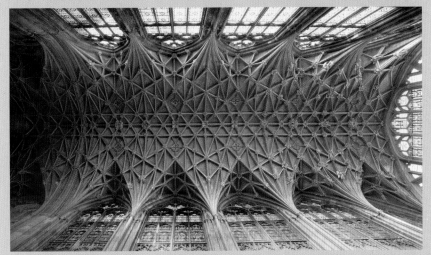

Region: France and England
Period: Twelfth to mid thirteenth century
Characteristics: Plate tracery; Pointed arch; Rib vault; Flying buttress; Four-storey bay; Sexpartite vault

The innovations of the choir at Saint-Denis quickly spread, and were applied and developed in successive cathedrals across the Île-de-France and further afield, notably in England. The essentially Romanesque three-storey bay of Saint-Denis was soon superseded by the addition of a triforium level above the gallery at Noyon Cathedral. The inclusion of this arcade often resulted in alternating major and minor piers and supports, which gave a sense of increased height and verticality over the more static Romanesque arrangement.

The vaulting system that characterized Early Gothic was sexpartite, that is, a vault divided into six parts by two diagonal ribs and one transverse rib. At Noyon and Laon, for example, each vault spans two arcade bays, as defined by the arches of the lower arcade, with the transverse vault running between the two adjacent bays across the nave. The apparent movement eastwards from the nave through the crossing to the chancel, while enhanced by the narrower bays created by the pointed arch, was mediated by the wide, almost square vaults above.

While Early Gothic cathedrals in France achieved a spatial unity and harmony, those in England in the style dubbed 'Early English' (roughly dating to between 1180 and 1275) retained a more additive, 'sum-of-their-parts' quality. The early choir at Canterbury was designed by a Frenchman (William of Sens) and for that reason can hardly be called English Gothic. Yet as the Gothic spread to Wells, Somerset, and to Lincoln in the 1190s, English masons adapted the style for their own ends. The arcade bays at Wells and Lincoln are wider than their French counterparts, and their vaults sit on corbels above the piers of the lower gallery rather than extending through them from the arcade below. Begun in 1220 and finished (apart from its façade and spire) comparatively quickly in 1258, Salisbury in Wiltshire is the most consistent example of the 'Early English' style: a tall, wide arcade; a plate-traceried gallery with a traditional lancet-windowed clerestory; and an elegantly light quadripartite vault soaring above.

Plate tracery

One of the earliest types of Gothic tracery, plate tracery seems to cut through a solid stone wall, creating a robust architectural effect that is usually loosely geometric rather than overtly decorative in appearance. It is far simpler than later forms of tracery, which are used to fill in an already-existing open space.

Salisbury Cathedral, Wiltshire, England, begun 1220

Pointed arch

The central feature of Gothic architecture, the pointed arch is formed from two (or more) intersecting curves that meet in a central apex or point. Their main structural advantage over the round arch is to enable greater height and the creation of rectangular bays.

Rib vault

A Romanesque groin vault (produced by the perpendicular intersection of two barrel vaults) is a structural whole; no part can be removed without its overall integrity being affected. The structural framework of a rib vault, in contrast, is produced by projecting strips of masonry – the ribs – which then support the 'web' or infill.

Cathedral Basilica of Saint-Denis, Paris, begun ca. 1135

Cathedral Basilica of Saint-Denis, Paris, begun ca. 1135

Flying buttress

Although they can be found in Romanesque
architecture, the possibilities of flying
buttresses were fully realized only with
the advent of the Gothic. They consist
of 'flying' (or open) half arches that help
counter the thrust of a high vault, allowing
higher buildings but without an increased
wall thickness.

Notre Dame, Paris, begun 1163

Four-storey bay

The earliest type of Gothic bay elevation, as seen at Saint-Denis, had three storeys. However, this was essentially an adaptation of the Romanesque and it quickly gave way to the four-storey bay, for example at Noyon, which consisted of arcade, gallery, triforium and clerestory.

Sexpartite vault

Romanesque architecture made use of simple barrel and groin vaults. The sexpartite vault, in many ways a natural progression from these types of vault, spans a square space and is divided into six parts by two diagonal ribs and one transverse rib.

Noyon Cathedral, Picardy, France, begun ca. 1131

Notre Dame, Paris, begun 1163

31

Region: Europe, especially France and England
Period: Thirteenth to mid fourteenth century
Characteristics: Three-storey bay; Height; Quadripartite vault; Bar tracery; Rose window; Decoration

It is arguably the great cathedral at Chartres, France, that marks the shift from the Early Gothic to the High Gothic style. Earlier cathedrals had made use of the sexpartite vault, creating essentially square bays. Rebuilt after a fire of 1194, Chartres simplified the sexpartite vault; the transverse ribs across each bay were removed so that the vault became quadripartite. The bays, therefore, more or less halve in width and become rectangular, increasing their frequency and the resultant speed at which the eye is drawn eastwards down the nave.

The other innovation at Chartres was a return to the three-storey bay elevation, but in reconfigured form. The gallery was removed from the four-storey arrangement, leaving just a low triforium dividing the tall arcade and clerestory levels. This simplified arrangement, with shaft piers beginning in the arcade, meant that the eye was drawn up through the arcade to the clerestory to the vault above. The overall effect of this arrangement, combined with the narrower bays, was to accentuate the horizontal and especially vertical dynamism.

Early Gothic cathedrals tended to treat a wall as a solid surface that was punched through with pointed-arched windows. In the High Gothic the effect is reversed. The pointed arch becomes the starting point. The columns are thinner, the moulding deeper, and the space itself seems to be constructed by the arch's repetition and articulation. First at Reims and then soon after at Amiens, Early Gothic plate tracery was replaced with bar tracery. Bar tracery was built up within each pointed-arch aperture with complex geometrical patterns filled with coloured glass. The overall effect was far more decorative than the comparatively austere Early Gothic cathedrals, and in England the High Gothic is known as the Decorated phase. Combined with ornate pinnacles and more complex patterns and mouldings, the new Decorated traceries created bold edifices for the east end of Lincoln Cathedral, the west front of York Minster, and the crossings of the cathedrals at Ely and Bristol.

Three-storey bay

By excluding the gallery from the four-storey bay elevation, a far clearer and unencumbered progression upwards could be created. The triforium arcade became a consistent horizontal band between arcade and clerestory uniting adjacent bays along the internal elevation.

Amiens Cathedral, Picardy, France, begun 1220

Height

High Gothic cathedrals were considerably higher, and the ratio of nave width to height larger, than those of the Early Gothic period. The nave at Noyon stood 26 metres (85 feet) high, while at Notre Dame, Paris, it rose to 35 metres (115 feet), at Reims 38 metres (125 feet), at Amiens 43 metres (140 feet) and at Beauvais a massive 48 metres (157 feet).

Beauvais Cathedral, Picardy, begun 1225

Quadripartite vault

The quadripartite vault, which omitted
the transverse ribs across the nave, was
simpler and more dynamic than the earlier
sexpartite vault. Bays no longer had to be
square, and could thereby nearly double
in number in an equivalent space.

Bar tracery

Unlike earlier plate tracery, which appeared
to cut through a solid wall, bar tracery
filled in an open space in the wall. This
allowed the designer far more freedom in
the choice of geometric pattern. Recurring
forms appearing in bar-traceried windows
included foils, daggers and mouchettes,
all arranged in a variety of patterns.

Chartres Cathedral, Eure-et-Loire,
France, begun 1194

West front, York Minster, Yorkshire,
England, ca. 1280–1350

Rose window

Circular windows had existed in
Romanesque and Early Gothic architecture.
There they tended to be relatively simple
'wheel' windows, formed by a number of
thick bars radiating from a small central
aperture. The advent of bar tracery resulted
in more intricate, petal-like designs at
Chartres and Laon, and later at Notre Dame.

Decoration

High Gothic was, on the whole, far
more decorated than Early Gothic. Piers
consisted of composite columns and had
deeper mouldings. Bar tracery included
such features as crockets, ball flowers,
diaper pattern and intricate foliation,
and, combined with figurative sculpture,
created a far more ornate architectural
effect – which in England is known as the
Decorated style.

South rose window, Notre Dame,
Paris, begun ca. 1258

Reims Cathedral, Marnes, France,
begun 1211

Region: Europe, especially Spain, Germany and England
Period: Mid fourteenth to fifteenth century
Characteristics: Intense ornamentation; Complex vaults; Lanterns; Ogee arch; Spatial unity; Perpendicular

The beginnings of the Late Gothic, here encompassing a number of geographical variations of the style, can be traced broadly to about 1300. It continued until the onset of the Renaissance, in some countries as late as 1500. Unlike in earlier iterations of the Gothic, no specific building can be identified as inaugurating the style. Rather, the overarching spatial integrity achieved in the High Gothic through elevation and vault, perhaps most perfectly at Reims and Amiens, gave way in the Late Gothic to an interest in surface effects. Piers become thinner, and their moulding more intricate; tracery patterns discarded any residual rigidity to become cobwebs of intersecting lines; vaults become more complex, yet appear lighter; and the spatial distinctions so integral to the High Gothic melt away, drawing the eye in far more directions.

High Gothic continued – and perfected – the ancient basilican form of a high nave with lower aisles on either side. One of the key advances of Late Gothic was to transcend this form, so that the nave and aisles are essentially one space with wider bays and ribs flowing apparently in all directions; this is seen, for example, in the dramatic choir of St. Lawrence in Nuremberg, Germany. Similarly, although in reverse, an aisleless nave was added in 1416 to a century-old French-style chancel with ambulatory and radiating chapels at Girona Cathedral, Spain. The width of the nave matched that of the ambulatory and apse combined. The overall feeling in both German and Spanish examples is of an overwhelming spatial complexity, further heightened by the proclivity in these two regions for dense layers of ornamentation.

The Gothic in England took a different direction to those of its European counterparts. From about 1350 a style now known as Perpendicular began to emerge. Elaborate tracery patterns were eschewed in favour of an apparently rational system of vertical and horizontal bars, creating series of repeating glazed panels. The complex vaults of the Decorated period evolved into the structurally simpler (though more dramatic in its apparent lightness) fan vault, formed from identical ribs emanating from a single point. The vaults of Gloucester Cathedral and the naves of Canterbury and Winchester cathedrals are among the most important realizations of the Perpendicular phase of Gothic. However, the numerous fifteenth-century royal commissions such as King's College Chapel, Cambridge, and Henry VII's chapel at Westminster Abbey, London, are without doubt its most singularly coherent achievements.

Intense ornamentation

While High Gothic turned towards greater spatial rationalism, Late Gothic was marked by a concern for surface with thinner, lighter and more intricate tracery. Iberian Gothic featured the most intense surface ornamentation, while the hardly less ornate German iteration retained a more spacious character.

San Pablo, Valladolid, Spain, begun 1445

Complex vaults

The quadripartite vault of the High Gothic phase was developed in a number of ways. Tierceron vaults featured additional ribs emanating from the main supports to abut on to the transverse ribs, sometimes with lierne ribs between them. In England this evolved into the fan vault, one of the main characteristics of the Perpendicular.

Choir, Gloucester Cathedral, Gloucestershire, England, 1331–55

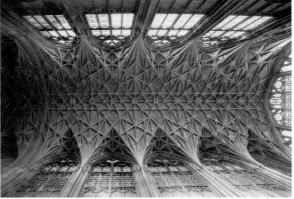

Lanterns

The form and proportions of Early and High Gothic cathedrals were essentially defined by the right angle. The Late Gothic was characterized by attempts at more complex spatial configurations, often realized in octagonal lanterns, for example at Ely, Cambridgeshire, and St. Ouen, Rouen, which gave dynamism to the traditionally static crossing.

Ogee arch

The ogee arch is a pointed arch, each side of which is composed of a lower concave curve intersecting a higher convex one. It is probably Moorish in origin but became a feature of the Late Gothic. It first appears at St. Urbain in Troyes, France, in the 1260s, but is most prevalent in the fourteenth century, particularly in Spain.

Spire, St. Ouen, Rouen, France,
1490–1515

Santa Maria, Requena, Spain,
fourteenth century

Spatial unity

Early and High Gothic cathedrals retained
the Romanesque basilican form with high
nave and lower aisles. Perhaps inspired by
the churches of Dominican and Franciscan
friars, Late Gothic cathedrals tended
towards more unified spaces with nave and
aisles of similar height, for example at Albi,
France, or St. Catherine in Barcelona.

Perpendicular

From about 1350 English Gothic began
to forego the complex tracery of the
Decorated phase in favour of an emphasis
on vertical and horizontal lines – hence the
name Perpendicular given to this phase.
The east window at Gloucester Cathedral is
one of the first instances of the style, a 'wall
of glass' defined by transoms and mullions.

Choir, St. Lawrence, Nuremberg,
Germany, begun 1445

Choir, Gloucester Cathedral,
Gloucestershire, 1331–55

Region: Venice, Italy
Period: Twelfth to fifteenth century
Characteristics: Polychromy; Arcades and balconies; Campanile; Ogee arch; Brick and stucco; Byzantine influence

During the Middle Ages Venice became an extremely wealthy and powerful city–state. Its strategically important location on the Adriatic Sea led to its control of trade routes between East and West, secured by a mighty navy. During the period of the Crusades (1095–1291) in particular, its naval power enabled it to acquire territories across the Adriatic, numerous Greek islands including Crete and, later, to reach Cyprus.

Key to Venice's military and commercial success was its stable political system, derived from its status as a Republic. The head of state was the Doge, who was elected for life (though sometimes forced to resign if he was unsuccessful or unpopular). Various councils acted as a check on the Doge's power, and some had the power of veto over his actions. Although complex and often fractious, the Venetian form of government ensured that all citizens – from aristocracy to merchants and the ordinary people – had a voice and a stake in Venice's wellbeing.

Shaped by these political, commercial and geographical particularities, Venetian Gothic was *sui generis*, unlike all other forms of Gothic architecture, even Italian Gothic, which resisted the emphasis on verticality of its northern counterparts and remained far plainer

(perhaps except for Milan's great cathedral). In any case, given Venice's location on a collection of marshy islands, certain building methods and materials – and therefore forms – had to be adapted. The use of arcades and balconies, most famously in the Doge's Palace, mitigated the impact of frequent floods. Brick, being lighter than stone and more tolerant of movement, was the predominant structural material. Covering buildings with expensive marble, mosaics and even gold on their publicly visible canal-facing fronts demonstrated their owners' wealth and status.

Venice's trading links with and comparative accessibility to the Byzantine and Islamic worlds led to cultural and, especially, architectural exchange too. The ogee arch, for example, usually found only in the Late Gothic in the rest of Europe, is common in Venetian Gothic (though not in ecclesiastical contexts). Spoliation from the East was also frequent, perhaps the most famous example being the four bronze horses looted from Constantinople in 1206 during the Fourth Crusade, which (until their replacement by replicas in the 1980s) looked out over St. Mark's Square from atop the basilica.

Polychromy

The most famous secular building in Venice, other than the Doge's Palace, is probably the Ca' d'Oro (House of Gold), with its lustrous marble facing, delicate mosaics and, of course, profusion of gold. Though rarely as sumptuous as in this example, this type of surface decoration was a key characteristic of Venetian Gothic.

Arcades and balconies

With flooding a yearly occurrence, almost all Venetian *palazzi* are built on tall arcades supporting the principal apartments. The arcade motif is usually carried through the storeys above, often with intricate openwork (unglazed tracery), for example at the Ca' Foscari.

Ca' d'Oro, Venice, 1428–30

Ca' Foscari, Venice, 1453

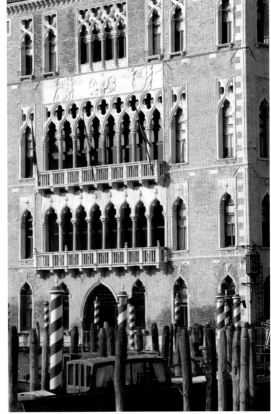

Campanile

A general feature of Italian architecture, campaniles (freestanding bell-towers) stand alongside most Venetian churches, the most famous being that in St. Mark's Square, originally medieval but rebuilt after its collapse in 1902. Another distinctive component of Venice's skyline is the flared chimney pots, the shape of which was intended to prevent the spread of fire.

St. Mark's Campanile, Venice, begun after 1489 with subsequent major alterations

Ogee arch

While usually only seen in Western Europe in Late Gothic architecture, the ogee arch appears frequently in Venetian Gothic buildings. Because of its probable origin in Islamic architecture, it was rarely used in ecclesiastical buildings, but instead was reserved for *palazzi*, such as the Palazzo Contarini-Fasan.

Palazzo Contarini-Fasan, Venice, fifteenth century

Brick and stucco

Constructed on marshy lagoon islands, most Venetian buildings stand on wooden piles sunk into the mud. Stone was, therefore, rarely extensively used. Local red brick is the most common material as it is relatively light and more tolerant of movement. It is often stuccoed and sometimes dressed with Istrian stone.

Byzantine influence

Venice's relative proximity to and strong trading links with the East, especially the Byzantine Empire, resulted in an important transfer of architectural ideas. The pendentive dome, for example, defines St. Mark's Basilica, which in essence is a Byzantine church. Frequent spoliation from the east also occurred, backed by the mighty Venetian navy.

Frari, Venice, 1250–1338

St. Mark's Basilica, Venice, begun ca. 1063

Region: Europe, especially northern regions
Period: Twelfth to fifteenth century
Characteristics: Wooden-framed ceilings; Arcades; Towers and turrets; Irregular plans; Oriel windows; (Pseudo) battlements

Through all its phases the Gothic was rarely confined solely to ecclesiastical architecture. Manor-houses, palaces and, especially, town halls and guildhalls employed the Gothic in grand and innovative ways, often quite distinct from its use in ecclesiastical contexts. The requirements of these building types were in a large part determined by medieval social and economic structures. As their positions became more secure, the nobility moved from often dank and uncomfortable castles into domestic residences. The consequent emergence of new typologies, in the English manor-house, the French château and the German schloss, provided new possibilities for architectural expression that borrowed and adapted elements of the Gothic from its ecclesiastical contexts. One direct link was the private chapel, an essential component of these new types of building.

In England, the manor-house was defined by its great hall, which was a place where secular authority was administered in the surrounding area. The hall had numerous uses: it was where the household dined, where the lord usually met and received guests, and even where some servants would have slept. Along with the chapel, the hall was usually the location for the house's richest architectural and heraldic display. Alongside a grand fireplace and wooden panelling, great timber ceilings often showed medieval craftsmanship and ingenuity at its finest.

The advent of international trade was also a defining characteristic of the medieval period. The transfer of goods had helped facilitate the transmission of architectural ideas, which had led to the establishment of the Gothic as a truly international style. Trade also led to the rise of architectural expressions of mercantile power – new exchanges, guildhalls and town halls – that were symbolic of civic as opposed to ecclesiastical authority. These new building types drew inspiration from both ecclesiastical and domestic architecture. Like the great cathedrals, many exchanges and halls in England, the Low Countries and for the Hanseatic League (the commercial association of cities in Northern Germany) were arranged around arcades that provided spaces for exchange of money and goods. Inside, without the need for extreme height, ceilings were often of timber, sometimes combined with masonry, for example in the Guildhall, London.

Wooden-framed ceilings

While the Gothic cathedral was characterized by its almost exclusively masonry vaulted ceilings, these are rarer in secular Gothic architecture, which tended to incorporate highly ornate timber-framed ceilings. One of the most famous in England is the great hammer-beamed ceiling of Middle Temple Hall, London.

Middle Temple Hall, London, begun 1562

Arcades

The cloth hall in Ypres is notable especially for its great arcade. The arcade is tailored to the requirements of this new commerce-oriented building type, yet maintains a symbolic link to the great cathedrals and their associations of power.

Cloth Hall, Ypres, Belgium, originally 1202–1304, reconstructed 1933–67

Towers and turrets

Many secular Gothic buildings had
important civic functions and were often
the symbolic architectural manifestation of
a town's status and ambition. Towers and
turrets, housing clocks, bells or staircases,
ensured that the building they adorned
was highly visible and dominated its
surrounding area.

Town Hall, Bruges, Belgium, 1376–1420

Irregular plans

The symmetry of the cruciform Gothic
cathedral plan was derived from particular
liturgical requirements, and also the
obvious symbolic significance of the
Latin cross form. Without such need for
symmetry, the designers of many Secular
Gothic buildings paid little attention to
it; scale and decoration were of greater
importance to them.

Penshurst Place, Kent, England, begun 1341

Oriel windows

The oriel window (named after Oriel College, Oxford) is one that projects from one or more upper storeys but does not extend to the ground floor. Along with the bay window (a projecting window that does reach the ground floor), it was a frequent feature in secular Gothic, especially buildings in the English Perpendicular style.

(Pseudo) battlements

The new building types of the English manor-house, the French château and the German schloss emerged from the reduced need for defence. However, the symbolic power and historic significance of defensive features such as battlements was not forgotten, and they frequently appear as decorative elements.

Front Quad, Oriel College, Oxford, England, 1620–2

Château d'Azay-le-Rideau, Loire Valley, France, 1518–27

Region: Europe
Period: Twelfth to fifteenth century
Characteristics: Battlements; Gatehouse; Towers; Bastions; Keep or donjon; Concentric curtain walls

A castle is the fortified residence of a lord or noble. The earliest examples were usually built of wood on top of large earthworks. This construction method had its origins long in the past; the earliest forts appeared once civilizations had accumulated enough wealth to make it worth protecting. However, the medieval castle, a residence as well as a fort, was quite different to the much earlier building type, and became inextricably linked to the feudal system. As monarchs devolved power at a local level to lords and knights, secure and impressive buildings were required from which such authority could be administered.

The first feudal castles were of the motte-and-bailey variety. A square keep, or donjon, atop a large mound of earth – the motte – was the administrative heart of the castle, containing the great hall, the chapel and the lord's residence. For that reason it was the most heavily fortified part. Below the motte was the bailey, a larger enclosed area fortified by a surrounding stake fence or palisade (later a stone wall) above a ditch. The bailey contained stables, barracks, workshops kitchens and other service buildings required for the castle to sustain itself.

From the end of the twelfth century the Crusades fundamentally altered the course of castle design. Inspired by Saracen examples, European castles – Château Gaillard, France, begun in 1196 by Richard I, King of England (r. 1189–99) and Duke of Aquitaine, was arguably the first – began to adopt series of concentric curtain walls, reducing the reliance on the keep for defence, which eventually disappeared from castle design. Symmetry also became an important consideration; castles were laid out on a regular plan, with their concentric walls punctuated by evenly spaced towers and bastions. The Castel del Monte, one of a number of castles built in southern Italy in the mid thirteenth century by the Holy Roman Emperor Frederick II (r. 1220–50), remains the most complete example of this period. Its octagonal plan perhaps derives from ancient Roman precedent, but was also inspired by contemporary Gothic architecture.

The concentric castle type evolved features such as round towers, which were less vulnerable to attack. However, the advent of gunpowder, and especially of heavy cannon in the mid fifteenth century, marked the end of the castle as fort-residence. A new generation of permanent forts better able to withstand cannon fire became the primary means of defence, yet castles have retained their symbolic significance up to the present day.

Battlements

Castles were equipped with various forms
of battlement. Crenellations, regularly
spaced teeth-like projections on a wall,
were the most characteristic. They were
often combined with machicolations: holes
in the floor between corbels that allowed
defenders to drop objects and liquids on
attackers below.

Sirmione Castle, Brescia, Italy,
thirteenth century

Gatehouse

Entry into and out of the castle was
regulated through the gatehouse. As an
obvious point of weakness in the castle's
defences, a gatehouse was usually heavily
fortified with battlements as well as one or
more portcullises and often a drawbridge.
Some castles also included a barbican, a
secondary gatehouse in which attackers
could be trapped.

Kidwelly Castle, Carmarthenshire, Wales,
begun 1200

Towers

While the keep was essentially a squat tower, towers became significant in concentric castles, as they strengthened potential defensive weak spots. They afforded castle occupants wide views of the surrounding area and oncoming attackers – who would soon be faced by hails of arrows and other missiles.

Castel del Monte, Apulia, Italy, 1240s

Bastions

Long curtain walls could be potentially vulnerable to attack or undermining from close range because an attacker knew that he could only be repelled from front on. Curtain walls were therefore often punctuated by bastions, tower-like structures projecting from the wall plane that allowed defenders to repel attackers from the side too.

Ramparts of Aigues-Mortes, Camargue, France, begun 1289

Keep or donjon

In motte-and-bailey castles and early concentric castles, the keep or donjon was most heavily fortified part of the castle. The keep contained the lord's residence and was the administrative centre of the building and its surrounding area.

Keep, Norwich Castle, Norfolk, begun 1095

Concentric curtain walls

Originating in Crusader castles such as the famous Krak des Chevaliers, Syria, concentric castles removed the focus on the keep and allowed a more tactical form of defence. Defensive troops could move around the castle far more easily, while attackers who breached the outer ring would have to counter a second, higher ring before being able to overrun the castle.

Krak des Chevaliers, Syria, begun 1140s

Renaissance and Mannerism

The fourteenth-century poet and classical scholar Petrarch was the first to characterize the period following the fall of the Roman Empire as a 'Dark Age', marked by a decline in culture and learning. Instead of viewing the classical era as one of pagan barbarity, he saw great value in its cultural achievements and ascribed considerable importance to the study of its surviving texts. While medieval Scholasticism had held that truth was pre-ordained by God, thereby giving the Church great authority and instrumentalizing the pursuit of knowledge, Humanist thought, on which Petrarch was highly influential, valued learning for its own sake.

Rinascita

The Renaissance – the cultural manifestation of which was the return to ancient models of art, architecture and literature – is inextricably linked with the advent and development of Humanism. The *rinascita* (rebirth) of classical learning that, at its core, asserted the primacy of human agency over received doctrines had profound effects, not just in an intellectual sphere but also for social relations and patronage. Classical texts had, of course, not been forgotten during the medieval period, and in Italy in particular antiquity's physical ruins were never far from view. Yet the study of such texts was open only to the educated elite; Humanist learning, which encompassed poetry, philosophy and Ciceronian rhetoric, could be read as an important sign of social distinction. Centres of Humanist learning developed in several Italian city–states, and as art and architecture were considered among the 'liberal arts', artists and architects often sat in patrons' inner circles.

Leon Battista Alberti

The key figure of the Early Renaissance in Italy was Leon Battista Alberti (1404–72). His *Della pittura* (On Painting; 1436) and *De re aedificatoria* (On the Art of Building; 1454) are arguably the Renaissance's most significant treatises on art and architecture respectively. In the former, Alberti famously first articulated the principles of linear perspective then being explored by artists such as Masaccio and, a little later, Piero della Francesca. Usually credited to the architect and goldsmith Filippo Brunelleschi (1377–1446), its invention allowed artists to create the illusion of depth through the use of orthogonal lines centring on a single vanishing point. This almost scientific method was vitally important in establishing painting as an authentic intellectual pursuit; it also reflected a broad interest in essential Neoplatonic forms that came to the fore in Alberti's architectural treatise.

Alberti consciously modelled *De re aedificatoria* on the then recently rediscovered *De architectura*, a treatise of ten books by the Roman architect Vitruvius (active 46–30 BCE). Alberti's explication of the orders focused on their role within an overall proportional system, and he argued that architecture, like painting, had a fundamental basis in geometry. Alberti's ideal form was the circle, which he regarded as deriving from nature – an idea illustrated famously in Leonardo da Vinci's *Vitruvian Man* (ca. 1490). The geometric basis of architecture, Alberti argued, was manifested in the centralized plan, which embodied his idea of beauty as 'a harmony and concord of all the parts achieved in such a manner that nothing could be added or taken away or altered except for the worse'.

Of Alberti's built works the one that came closest to realizing his ideals was S. Sebastiano in Mantua, Italy. Yet, the design also reflects the need to reconcile Renaissance idealism with ecclesiastical requirements – an ongoing concern for Renaissance architects. Indeed, as the Renaissance progressed, architectural principles were increasingly codified, and architects soon began to manipulate them, thus heralding what is now known as Mannerism; meanwhile, as Renaissance ideas were dispersed, notably to northern Europe, they were adapted to reflect local contexts and traditions.

Early Renaissance

High Renaissance

Northern Renaissance

Mannerism

Region: Italy, especially Florence
Period: Fifteenth century
Characteristics: Centralized plan; Emulation of the Antique; Invention; Spatial harmony; Proportional façade; Delicacy

The rebuilding of Florence's ancient, crumbling cathedral had begun as early as 1296. Various figures, including the painter Giotto, were appointed over the course of the fourteenth century to oversee the project, and the design was enlarged several times as work progressed. By 1418, with much of the rest of the cathedral complete, the huge 42-metre-wide (138-foot-wide) crossing remained open. A competition was organized to find a solution for completing the crossing with a huge dome. The two most famous entrants were Filippo Brunelleschi and the goldsmith Lorenzo Ghiberti. A few years earlier, Ghiberti had triumphed over Brunelleschi in a competition to design the bronze doors of Florence's Baptistery. However, on this occasion, after much wrangling, Brunelleschi received the commission for what became the defining achievement of the Early Renaissance.

A decision had already been taken to reject Gothic flying buttresses for the design; Brunelleschi, therefore, had to look to ancient Rome for inspiration, and thereby marked a decisive and highly symbolic break with the Gothic past. The second-century Pantheon in Rome (see page 14) was the obvious model but it was a circular dome, rather than the octagonal shape required in

Florence; also, the Pantheon was built of concrete, the formula for which was long lost. Moreover, given the Florentine dome's huge scale, it wasn't possible to erect a temporary wooden support during its construction; it had to be self-supporting from the start. Brunelleschi created supporting ribs in each of the corners and a highly innovative solution to the problem of the dome 'spreading' under its own weight: an ingenious, self-supporting herringbone pattern was devised to spread the load of the bricks as soon as they were set.

Although the ribs of Brunelleschi's dome gave it a slightly Gothic appear–ance, in spirit, ambition and overt emulation of antiquity, it was wholly a product of the Renaissance. Brunelleschi looked to the Ancients in other ways too. In an arcade at the Ospedale degli Innocenti (Foundling Hospital) in Florence, begun in 1421, he deployed a distinctly classical language of slender Corinthian columns with pedimented windows above corresponding to the arched openings; spandrel medallions by Andrea della Robbia depicted the foundlings. Among the first Florentine buildings to use classical forms convincingly, it paved the way for a number of important works over succeeding decades.

Centralized plan

The Early Renaissance saw the first experiments with the Neoplatonic ideal of the centralized plan. Brunelleschi's S. Maria degli Angeli was begun in 1434, but left incomplete. Michelozzo's east end of SS. Annunziata, Florence, begun in 1444, is a complete example, but Giuliano da Sangallo the Elder's S. Maria delle Carceri is the most perfect of the early iterations.

Emulation of the Antique

In his incomplete Tempio Malatestiano in Rimini, Alberti attempted to employ the Roman triumphal arch motif in church architecture. He succeeded in doing so at the slightly later S. Andrea, Mantua, in which he used various Roman features, notably the coffered barrel vault, to reconcile its essentially longitudinal space with his preferred centralized ideal.

Giuliano da Sangallo the Elder, S. Maria delle Carceri, Prato, 1486–95

Leon Battista Alberti, S. Andrea, Mantua, begun 1470

Invention

Brunelleschi's dome is symbolic of Florence as the birthplace of the Renaissance. The spirit of creative invention in early fifteenth-century Florence was born from the coalescence of its political and social systems, finance and, most importantly, patrons such as the famous Cosimo de' Medici, whose Humanist interests led him to commission some of the period's greatest works of art.

Filippo Brunelleschi, Dome, Basilica di Sta. Maria del Fiore (Florence Cathedral), Florence, 1420–36

Spatial harmony

The flat roof and round windows of Brunelleschi's S. Spirito are vaguely Romanesque in derivation. Yet its arcade and volumes are the result of a deep understanding of the spatial harmony of classical architecture. The nave is twice as high as it wide, while in its entirety it is exactly four and a half cubes. The ground floor and clerestory are exactly equal in height.

Filippo Brunelleschi, S. Spirito, Florence, begun 1436

Proportional façade

The coherent proportional system of
Alberti's Palazzo Rucellai emerges from its
arrangement of the orders. Doric pilasters
at ground level, Ionic on the first floor
and Corinthian above frame the repeating
series of windows to give the whole façade
a sense of order, a principle Alberti also
deployed in the façade of S. Maria Novella
in Florence.

Leon Battista Alberti, Palazzo Rucellai,
Florence, begun 1446

Delicacy

In contrast to its heavily rusticated,
almost fortress-like exterior – security
was a necessity for such a rich and
controversial figure as Cosimo de' Medici –
the inner courtyard of Michelozzo's
Palazzo Medici is light and airy. Its slender
columns, characteristic of the Early
Renaissance, recall those of Brunelleschi's
Ospedale degli Innocenti, as well as much
earlier Florentine examples such as the
Romanesque S. Miniato (1062–90 and later).

Michelozzo di Bartolomeo Michelozzi,
courtyard, Palazzo Medici, Florence,
1445–60

Region: Italy
Period: Sixteenth century
Characteristics: Centralized plan; Plastic façade; Mastery of perspective; Emulation of the Antique; Monumentality; Grandeur

The shift from the Early to the High Renaissance was inaugurated arguably in one particular building: the Palazzo della Cancelleria in Rome, begun in 1486. Deploying Alberti's principles, the Cancelleria's unknown architect gives them an architectural expression beyond what Alberti was able to achieve in the Palazzo Rucellai. The ground level of the Cancelleria does away with an order on its regularly rusticated ground storey. Above, pilasters frame the windows but not in the simple rhythm used at the Rucellai; the gaps between pilasters that flank windows are wider than those that do not, giving the Cancelleria's façade a more ordered sense of grandeur. This is further accentuated by the slight projection of the end bays, which serve to terminate the façade elegantly. Each component has its own clearly articulated function within the façade; instead of simply resting on the cornice below, the windows are, for example, given proper sills at the base level of the pilasters.

The Cancelleria was built for Cardinal Raffaele Riario, a nephew of Pope Sixtus IV and it heralds Rome as the principal centre of the High Renaissance. It was under Pope Julius II, another nephew of Sixtus IV, that the defining architectural project of arguably the whole Renaissance was to begin: the rebuilding of St. Peter's. At the beginning of the sixteenth century St. Peter's was still essentially the basilica founded by the Emperor Constantine (see page 16) in the early fourth century, and was increasingly falling into ruin. In 1506 Julius II commissioned Donato Bramante (1443/4–1514) to rebuild the cathedral, fit for a new age.

Bramante was born near Urbino, and like many of the leading figures of the Roman Renaissance, including Raphael (1483–1520) and Michelangelo (1475–1564) – who would both also later work at St. Peter's – he had worked elsewhere before arriving in the Eternal City. Bramante's famous design was for a colossal centralized structure rather than a traditional longitudinal church, indicating just how far the Humanistic world view had permeated the Church. A hemispherical dome was intended to sit on four identical piers in a design of perfect symmetry and geometrical proportion. Bramante's dome was largely based on that of the Pantheon (see page 14) and reflected the vigour with which architects were increasingly drawing from the Antique. No longer was theory delicately put into practice; instead, grandeur and majesty became architects' overriding concerns.

Centralized plan

Although the centralized plan appeared
in the Early Renaissance (see page 55),
when artists and architects such as
Leonardo experimented with it both on
paper and in practice, it was perfected
in the High Renaissance in Bramante's
famous Tempietto of S. Pietro in Montorio,
which marks the precise location of
St. Peter's crucifixion. Bramante devised
a proportional system that defines the
whole structure and volume, a principle
he developed in his designs for St. Peter's.

Donato Bramante, Tempietto of S. Pietro in
Montorio, Rome, 1502

Plastic façade

Unlike in earlier *palazzi* in which the façade,
despite its architectural articulation, was
treated essentially as a flat surface or in low
relief, in the Palazzo Vidoni Caffarelli the
wall becomes plastic. Pilasters are replaced
by columns pushed together to operate
as pairs, their bases alternating with
window balconettes, while the ground-floor
rustication takes on a sculptural dimension.

Raphael, Palazzo Vidoni Caffarelli, Rome,
ca. 1515–20 (later altered and enlarged)

Mastery of perspective

Bramante's early S. Maria presso S. Satiro in Milan was clearly inspired by Alberti's S. Andrea in Mantua (see page 55), which Bramante must have studied in plan form as its construction was then still in its early stages. As there was no space for a chancel, Bramante used his deep knowledge of linear perspective to create one in illusion, complete with painted, coffered ceiling and columns diminishing in scale.

Emulation of the Antique

Commissioned from Raphael by Cardinal Giulio de' Medici, later Pope Clement VII, the Villa Madama and its circular courtyard were inspired by ancient Roman baths, notably those of Caracalla (see page 12). Its interior decoration, created by Giulio Romano, Baldassare Peruzzi and Giovanni da Udine, was based on surviving fragments from the ruins of the Emperor Nero's first-century Domus Aurea (Golden House).

Donato Bramante, S. Maria presso
S. Satiro, Milan, 1478–86

Begun by Raphael, Villa Madama,
outside Rome, 1518–25

Monumentality

One of Michelangelo's first architectural works, the new sacristy at S. Lorenzo was commissioned by the Medici family as their mortuary chapel. Michelangelo created a highly architectonic space topped by a coffered pendentive dome. For the tombs, which he also designed, he sculpted monumental allegorical figures, the combined effect of which was designed to suggest the eternal power of the Medici dynasty.

Michelangelo, new sacristy, S. Lorenzo, Florence, 1520–24

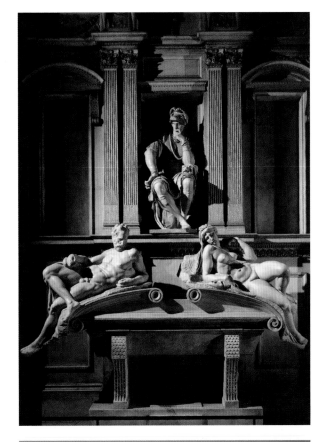

Grandeur

Redesigned by Antonio da Sangallo the Younger (1483–1546) in 1534, the Palazzo Farnese symbolizes the grandeur of the Roman High Renaissance. The façade eschews the usual ground-floor rustication apart from thick quoins, while its first-floor windows are topped by alternating triangular and segmental pediments, a Roman motif. Its heavy cornice and upper courtyard storey were added later in a Mannerist spirit by Michelangelo.

Antonio da Sangallo the Younger, Palazzo Farnese, Rome, 1534–46

Region: France, the Netherlands, England; also Germany and eastern Europe
Period: Sixteenth century
Characteristics: Local traditions; Symmetry; Medieval plan; Animated skyline; Emblematism; Authenticity

The advent of the printing press in the fifteenth century enabled the dispersal of architectural ideas far wider and more quickly than ever before. The most influential in northern Europe was the treatise *Tutte l'opere d'architettura, et prospetiva* (Complete Works on Architecture and Perspective) by Sebastiano Serlio (1475–1554). Born in Bologna and trained initially as a painter, Serlio had worked with the Baldassare Peruzzi (1481–1536) in Rome until the city was sacked by mutinous troops of the Holy Roman Emperor in 1527. Fleeing to Venice, there Serlio remained until 1540 when he was brought to Fontainebleau by the French King Francis I (r. 1515–47) to assist in the building of his great château. Only the Porte Dorée at Fontainebleau survives of what may reliably be attributed to Serlio; his most enduring impact, in any case, was on paper. His treatise, published in several parts between 1537 and 1575, focused on the practical rather than theoretical aspects of Renaissance architecture, while its numerous illustrations, including for the first time of the five orders, provided models ready to be copied.

Despite increasing familiarity with Renaissance ideas – the French trio of Philibert de l'Orme, Jean Bullant and Pierre Lescot all visited Rome in the 1530s, for example – for much of the sixteenth century classical forms and motifs were employed in northern Europe in an emblematic manner. Classical elements typically augmented, rather than replaced, established architectural languages, and the fundamental ordering principles of classical architecture were largely eschewed in favour of continuing use of traditional forms. Classical experiments were often confined to funerary monuments or to additions to existing structures such as the gatehouse (ca. 1555) by Bullant for the château at Écouen. Lescot's work at the Louvre, Paris, from the mid sixteenth century remains among the first instances in northern Europe of classical principles being used to order a façade that is then ornamented with traditional motifs, rather than the other way round.

The French and also Dutch examples were influential on the large number of great houses constructed in England during the reign (1558–1603) of Elizabeth I. So-called prodigy houses, such as Burghley House in Cambridgeshire, Longleat House in Wiltshire and Hardwick Hall in Derbyshire, were symmetrical, in some instances quite innovative in plan and made often relatively correct use of classical ornament, yet maintained strong continuities with the English Perpendicular tradition; indeed, in spirit and appearance they have more in common with English houses of 100 years earlier than any Italian prototype. It was only in the early seventeenth century, with the work of Inigo Jones (1573–1652), that an authentically Italianate form of classical architecture became established in England.

Local traditions

Serlio's Château d'Ancy-le-Franc reflects
both Renaissance principles and local
traditions. Pilasters order the plain but
otherwise classical façade and corner
pavilions. The steeply pitched roof, gable
windows and tower-like corner pavilions,
however, keep the building's appearance
largely within the realms of French
architectural tradition.

Sebastiano Serlio, Château d'Ancy-le-Franc,
Burgundy, France, 1544–50

Symmetry

In medieval domestic architecture
symmetry was rarely considered to be
important, and buildings were constructed
largely in an additive, piecemeal fashion.
However, the influence of Renaissance
planning principles saw symmetry
become increasingly significant as a
guiding architectural principle, even
when the building's articulation oscillated
between the classical and Gothic, as at
Hardwick Hall.

Robert Smythson, Hardwick Hall, Derbyshire,
England, 1590–97

Medieval plan

One of the grandest English houses of
its day, Kirby Hall essentially followed a
medieval plan, with the main focus on
the great hall and a courtyard surrounded
by wings, the rooms within arranged
consecutively. Classical motifs, including
giant pilasters derived from the work of
Michelangelo, are used emblematically to
decorate the elevations of this otherwise
traditional building.

Thomas Thorpe (attributed), Kirby Hall,
Northamptonshire, England, 1570–72

Animated skyline

In plan, the Château de Chambord, with its large, round corner towers, appears most akin to a castle. However, in elevation those towers are cut through with large windows and articulated with pilasters. Its skyline, especially the central section, is a riot of competing towers and turrets, largely Gothic in form but draped in all manner of classical ornament.

Domenico da Cortona, Château de Chambord, Loire, France, 1519–47

Emblematism

Architectural treatises were often used as pattern books by masons looking to adorn otherwise traditional buildings with novel classical forms. In buildings such as the Stadhuis (Town Hall) in Antwerp, the orders are used in an emblematic manner, ornamenting a relatively traditional building form rather than determining the building's organizing principles.

Cornelis Floris de Vriendt, Stadhuis, Antwerp, Belgium 1561–5

Authenticity

On some occasions, patrons in northern Europe were amenable to Renaissance ideas from early on; Henry VII's tomb in Westminster Abbey, London, was designed by the sculptor Pietro Torrigiano who had famously broken Michelangelo's nose while both were apprenticed in Florence. Yet, it was with Inigo Jones that Italianate classical architecture gained a foothold in England; his Banqueting House was the seed from which, he hoped, a new Whitehall Palace would emerge.

Inigo Jones, Banqueting House, London, begun 1619–22

Region: Italy, and also Spain
Period: Mid to late sixteenth century
Characteristics: Austerity; Undulating façade; Solids and voids; Differing rhythms; Ambiguity; Piety

In his *Le Vite de' piu eccellenti pittori, scultori, e architettori* (Lives of the Artists), first published in 1550, the painter, architect and writer Giorgio Vasari (1511–74) was among the first to describe the artistic accomplishments of the fifteenth and sixteenth centuries in terms of a *rinascita* (rebirth) or Renaissance. The book, which he revised and republished in 1568, charted the progression of the arts from the Florentine painter Cimabue in the thirteenth century towards a golden age of the early sixteenth century embodied by Leonardo, Raphael and, above all, Michelangelo. 'Everything [Leonardo] does', Vasari wrote, 'comes from God rather than from human art', while Raphael 'was endowed by nature with the goodness and modesty to be found in all those exceptional men'. The genius of Michelangelo, Vasari observed, was able to surpass the beauty of nature itself; indeed, God himself had sent 'an artist who would be skilled in each and every craft … and, in architecture, create buildings which would be comfortable and secure, healthy, pleasant to look at, well-proportioned and richly ornamented'.

Faced with the scale of these artists' achievements, and as classical systems and architectural theory were formalized in treatises, architects became increasingly self-conscious in the way they adapted or broke the established rules, creating works now described as Mannerist. Yet the first signs of Mannerism appeared in the singularly restless work of Michelangelo, whose Biblioteca Laurenziana in Florence arguably inaugurated the style. Michelangelo's Mannerism is most visible in his designs for St. Peter's. Called upon by Pope Paul III in 1546 to take over the repeatedly stalled rebuilding, Michelangelo went back to Bramante's original designs, which in the intervening years had been augmented by Raphael, Baldassare Peruzzi and Antonio da Sangallo the Younger. Michelangelo simplified Bramante's plan, enlarging the four central piers to truly epic proportions, and removing the secondary radiating centres to create a single massive ambulatory. Stairwells placed in the corners of the transepts created an undulating external wall surface, emphasized by overlapping pilasters set at opposing angles. The heavy attic storey mixed aedicules with oblong windows, apparently turned on their sides with elaborate architectonic 'hoods', while the absence of a cornice draws the eye up to the dome above – an extraordinarily autonomous and archetypal Mannerist statement.

Austerity

Mannerism was by no means confined
to Italy. The gridiron courtyard plan of
the El Escorial palace complex outside
Madrid built by Philip II, King of Spain
(r. 1554–98) is almost certainly based on
antique models. Its plain Mannerist exterior
reflected both the difficulty of carving the
local stone and a preference for an austere
form of classicism that Philip regarded as
reflecting his intense religious faith.

Juan Bautista de Toledo and Juan de Herrara,
El Escorial, outside Madrid, Spain, 1559–84

Undulating façade

The Palazzo Massimo alle Colonne by the Sienese architect Baldassare Peruzzi moves beyond even the plastic façade of Raphael's High Renaissance Palazzo Vidoni Caffarelli, also in Rome (see page 59). Its curving façade is curiously flat, and contrasts starkly with the dark ground-floor loggia, while its windows have thin, quite oddly articulated surrounds, which puncture the rustication in staccato fashion.

Baldassare Peruzzi, Palazzo Massimo alle Colonne, Rome, 1532–6

Solids and voids

The most influential architect in the history of Western architecture, Andrea Palladio (1508–80) developed a very personal Mannerist style. In the Palazzo Chiericati, one of a number of *palazzi* and villas in the Veneto for which he is best known, he used the form of a courtyard colonnade from a Roman house to create the façade. Its alternating solids and voids are a key Mannerist architectural effect.

Andrea Palladio, Palazzo Chiericati, Vicenza, begun 1550

Differing rhythms

A pupil of Raphael, Giulio Romano (1499–1546) was one of the leading Mannerists, completing several notable works in Mantua where he was employed by the court of the Gonzaga Dukes of Mantua. The Palazzo del Te is his masterpiece; the complexity of its exquisite illusionistic frescoes inside is heralded by the differing and, in some ways, competing rhythms of its façades.

Giulio Romano, Palazzo del Te, Mantua, 1525–35

Ambiguity

Michelangelo's second architectural
work after the new sacristy at S. Lorenzo,
the Biblioteca Laurenziana embodies the
formal ambiguity that defined Mannerism.
Among the many Mannerist devices in this
building are the pairs of columns repeated
around the vestibule and recessed into
the wall rather than applied to its surface;
the corbels below add to the apparent
structural uncertainty.

Piety

Founded in 1540 just before the epochal
Council of Trent (see page 70), the Society
of Jesus (the Jesuits) figured centrally in
the Counter-Reformation, and their Il Gesù
church was among the movement's first
cultural manifestations. Reverting to a
longitudinal plan, it follows the Albertian
precedent of aisles configured as side-
chapels, but here they become more or
less niches off a vast open nave.

Michelangelo, Biblioteca Laurenziana,
Florence, 1524

Giacomo Vignola and Giacomo della Porta,
Il Gesù, Rome, 1568–84

Baroque and Rococo

The Baroque was arguably the first truly international architectural style. Emerging in Rome in the first years of the seventeenth century before spreading to Spain, France, Germany and later England, it reached as far as Scandinavia, Russia and even Latin America. Although manifestations of the Baroque differed according to location and architect, illusion and drama are traditionally seen as its principal characteristics. Extending the classical forms of the Renaissance (see page 52), the Baroque was characterized by bold and powerful massing, sweeping curves, dramatic effects of light and shade, and sumptuous, highly decorated interiors that blurred the boundaries between architecture, painting and sculpture.

The term Baroque derives from the French word for a misshapen or deformed pearl. For many later scholars, this connotation of trammelled beauty cast Baroque art and architecture as 'degenerate' and barely worthy of study. For the influential nineteenth-century cultural historian Jacob Burckhardt, the Baroque reflected a subversion of the values of the Renaissance. However, it was Burckhardt's pupil, the great architectural historian Heinrich Wölfflin, who first gave the Baroque serious scholarly attention; his influential *Renaissance und Barock* (1888) explored Baroque architecture in direct relation to that of the Renaissance.

The Counter-Reformation

Although Wölfflin was an avowed formalist, he did admit that it was impossible to separate an understanding of the Baroque from its historical context of the Counter-Reformation. A direct response to the Protestant Reformation of the early sixteenth century, led by Martin Luther, the Counter-Reformation sought to reassert the supremacy of the Roman Catholic faith through the consolidation and renewal of its fundamental tenets. Edicts issued by the Council of Trent, which first convened in 1545, imposed tight controls governing the iconography and style of religious art. This revitalization of the Church permeated into architecture, and a renewed vigour and confidence characterized many church commissions

of the seventeenth century, particularly the works of Gian Lorenzo Bernini (1598–1680) and Francesco Borromini (1599–1667). Buildings such as Sant'Andrea al Quirinale and San Carlo alle Quattro Fontane, both in Rome, appeal directly to the emotions. Their sheer scale and opulent decoration, combining architecture with painting and sculpture, were highly visible reminders of the power and prestige of the Roman Catholic Church.

International Baroque

The Baroque spread throughout Europe, and reached Protestant areas, notably northern Germany, the centre of Martin Luther's religious uprising. Here, however, it was less dramatic, in stark contrast to the sumptuous Bohemian Baroque of Johann Balthasar Neumann (1687–1753) and Johann Bernhard Fischer von Erlach (1656–1723) to the south. As the Protestant religion placed less emphasis on purpose-built churches, it was in palace architecture that the Baroque reached its zenith in many parts of Europe, as a manifestation of power.

In Protestant England, insulated both by geography and religion from continental Europe, the Baroque developed later in an idiosyncratic and short-lived form. The great houses of Castle Howard, North Yorkshire, and Blenheim Palace, Oxfordshire, designed by Sir John Vanbrugh (1664–1726) in collaboration with Nicholas Hawksmoor (1661–1736), the inspired pupil of Sir Christopher Wren (1632–1723), aimed at the scale of Louis XIV's palace at Versailles, near Paris. In style, however, they drew on models less representative of absolutist rule: the villas of the sixteenth-century Italian architect Andrea Palladio (see page 68) in their plans, and the native medieval and Elizabethan traditions in their handling of form and mass. The apotheosis of the Baroque in England was perhaps in Hawksmoor's London churches, six brooding edifices of white stone.

The Baroque's legacy was, as later architectural historians described it, the idea of a building as *Gesamtkunstwerk* – a total work of art – which the designers of the Rococo, the final, subversive stage of the Baroque, often took to decorative extremes.

Italian Baroque

German and Eastern
European Baroque

Spanish and Latin
American Baroque

French Baroque

English Baroque

Rococo

Region: Italy
Period: Seventeenth and eighteenth centuries
Characteristics: Oblique angles; Ovals; Curving façades; Giant order; Synthesis of architecture and sculpture; Illusion

The Baroque in Italy was first heralded in Michelangelo's dome of St. Peter's in Rome. In place of Bramante's planned hemispherical dome (see page 58), Michelangelo envisaged a thrusting ovoid dome. Whether this was Michelangelo's final intention is still the subject of debate, as he died when only drum level had been reached. However, it was this steeper, more dynamic shape that more or less was executed under the supervision of Giacomo della Porta (ca. 1533–1602). Completed in 1590, it towers over Rome, proclaiming the style that was to define the city's – and, indeed, much of Italy's – architecture for the next century.

Michelangelo's Baroque remained exceptional in a period in which Mannerism was predominant. The Baroque really belonged to a later generation of architects, among whom Gian Lorenzo Bernini and Francesco Borromini stand apart. Along with Pietro da Cortona (1596–1669), the other great exponent of the Baroque in Rome, both architects came from outside the city where they made their names. Early in their careers all three had worked together on the Palazzo Barberini, which had been begun by Carlo Maderno (ca. 1556–1629) just before his death;

however, they went on to be fierce rivals, especially Bernini and Borromini.

As well as being an architect, Bernini was without doubt the greatest sculptor of the Baroque. Borromini, in contrast, trained as a mason and worked in that capacity at St. Peter's while Bernini created one of his great masterpieces: the huge, four-columned bronze baldacchino that sits beneath Michelangelo's dome. Bernini's work at St. Peter's extended to the external monumental colonnades, which dramatically frame Maderno's façade and Michelangelo's dome above.

Borromini's greatest work is on an altogether much smaller scale: his church of San Carlo alle Quattro Fontane. Its undulating façade prefigures the spatial complexity of the interior, where Borromini was able to conjure an almost tangible feeling of movement from the static masonry.

The Baroque spread from Rome to all parts of Italy and especially to Turin. There, in the hands of the architect–mathematician Guarino Guarini (1624–83), were realized some of its greatest expressions, most notably the extraordinary dome of S. Lorenzo and the sweeping façade of the Palazzo Corignano.

Oblique angles

Along with the oval, oblique angles are a defining element of Baroque architecture, especially that of the Modena-born Guarino Guarini. He was an eminent mathematician as well as an architect, and a deep under-standing of geometry pervades many of his works, most notably the extraordinary dome of S. Lorenzo in Turin.

Guarino Guarini, S. Lorenzo, Turin, 1666–80

Ovals

While the perfect symmetry of the circle epitomized the order of Renaissance architecture, the Baroque was characterized by the oval. It defines the domes of the twin churches of Santa Maria dei Miracoli and Santa Maria in Montesanto standing over the Piazza del Popolo, Rome; and, in Borromini's S. Carlo and Bernini's nearby Sant'Andrea al Quirinale, is the unifying element of the whole work of architecture.

Curving façades

If the effect of drama was one of the fundamental characteristics of the Baroque, then the curving façade was one of the principal means of achieving it. Pietro da Cortona's Sta. Maria della Pace is one of the most famous such façades of the Baroque; its convex centrepiece and concave wings almost recall a theatre set.

Gian Lorenzo Bernini, Sant'Andrea al Quirinale, Rome, 1658–70

Pietro da Cortona, Sta. Maria della Pace, Rome, 1656–67

Giant order

A giant column or pilaster is one that extends through two or more storeys. It has a strong emblematic and expressive quality. Bernini used it in his extraordinary colonnades for St. Peter's Square, Rome, and also, in Solomonic (scrolling) form, in his sumptuous baldacchino standing beneath Michelangelo's dome.

Synthesis of architecture and sculpture

Bernini's sculpture of the *Ecstasy of St. Teresa* in Sta. Maria della Vittoria in Rome sits in a perfectly crafted architectural setting. The Cornaro Chapel frames the sculpture with curving forms and rich marble, while sculpted onlookers complicate the boundary between the viewer and the supernatural vision of the scene beyond.

Gian Lorenzo Bernini, baldacchino, St. Peter's, Rome, 1623–34

Gian Lorenzo Bernini, *Ecstasy of St. Teresa*, Cornaro Chapel, Sta. Maria della Vittoria, Rome, 1647–52

Illusion

Spatial illusion pervades Bernini's Scala
Regia (1663–6) in the Vatican, where he
used the narrow plan to create a dynamic
space, punctuated by pools of light. The
Baroque also made frequent use of pictorial
illusion, for example in the frescoes by
Andrea Pozzo (1642–1709) in the church
of St. Ignatius of Loyola.

Andrea Pozzo, nave frescoes, St. Ignatius of Loyola,
Campus Martius, Rome, from 1685

Region: Germany and eastern Europe
Period: Seventeenth and eighteenth centuries
Characteristics: Italian influence; Palace architecture; Gothic influence; Synthesis of classical and sacred architecture; Spatial complexity; Onion dome

The Thirty Years War (1618–48), fought principally in and around the Holy Roman Empire, which then encompassed much of central and eastern Europe, delayed the spread of the Baroque to those areas. Building almost ceased entirely while the war was waged, and recovered only in the second half of the seventeenth century.

The Holy Roman Empire was actually a collection of territories, governed by various kings, princes, counts and even ecclesiastical authorities. Religious differences – essentially those between Roman Catholics and Protestants – had precipitated the war and would do much to shape the take-up of the Baroque. The number of states and their diversity in both governance and religion was reflected architecturally; there was not one Baroque but many.

An early and influential version of the Baroque was that developed in Vienna for the Habsburg imperial rulers by Johann Lukas von Hildebrandt (1668–1745) and especially Fischer von Erlach. The latter was particularly inspired by the work of Bernini, and adapted his sweeping curving forms to the architectural requirements of the Habsburg Holy Roman Emperors Joseph I (r. 1705–11) and his younger brother Charles VI (r. 1711–40), for whom he built the Karlskirche, which incorporated intriguing allusions to various aspects of architectural history.

Even within a single area of the Empire the architecture varied considerably. In Bavaria architects as different as the Asam brothers and Johann Balthasar Neumann were working at much the same time. The Asam brothers were craftsmen–sculptors turned architects, and their Bernini-inspired works were unsurprisingly marked by grand sculptural adornment.

Neumann, in contrast, was highly educated with a background in military engineering. The pink and gold interior of his masterpiece, the Basilica of the Vierzehnheiligen, near Bamberg, borders on the Rococo in its freedom, yet its genius lies in its extraordinary geometry. Neumann reconfigured the traditional nave–aisle–transept design into a series of ovals that intersect at various stages in the elevation, an effect appealing to the mind as much as the emotions.

An almost Gothic quality infuses some of Neumann's complex spatial arrangements. This characteristic is seen even more explicitly in some of the more eccentric creations of the Bohemian Baroque, especially those of Jan Santini-Aichel (1667–1723), and in the persistence of the medieval onion dome in eastern Europe.

Italian influence

Among Italian architects, Guarino Guarini
was the most influential on the Baroque
architecture of southern Germany
especially; no doubt this was due to the
proximity of Turin, site of his most famous
works and a centre for craftsmen able to
realize such elaborate visions. The works
of Bernini and Borromini were also an
important inspiration, especially for the
Asam brothers at Weltenburg.

Egid Quirin Asam and Cosmas Damian Asam,
Weltenburg, Bavaria, abbey church, 1717–21

Palace architecture

Given the number of states in the Holy
Roman Empire, palaces were frequently
comissioned from Baroque architects. Most
of these palaces, of which Hildebrandt's
Upper Belvedere in Vienna is a stunning
example, had long ranges articulated
with the giant order and a recessed
frontispiece, features that are largely
indebted to Louis XIV's great palace at
Versailles, France.

Johann Lukas von Hildebrandt,
Upper Belvedere, Vienna, 1717–23

Gothic influence

Jan Santini-Aichel was a Bohemian architect of Italian descent, as his name suggests. His distinctive approach is most vividly reflected in his Pilgrimage Church of St. John of Nepomuk, which reveals an idiosyncratic fusion of a Baroque curving façade and Gothic pointed-arch windows.

Jan Santini-Aichel, Pilgrimage Church of St. John of Nepomuk, Žd'ár nad Sázavou, Czech Republic, 1719–27

Synthesis of classical and sacred architecture

In 1713 the Holy Roman Emperor Charles VI undertook the building of a church to S. Carlo Borromeo in Vienna. Fischer von Erlach won the commission with an extraordinary design incorporating a frontage in the form of a Greek temple, Roman Baroque side pavilions and two columns modelled on Trajan's Column – an ensemble standing as the consummate expression of Charles VI's imperial might.

Johann Bernhard Fischer von Erlach, Karlskirche, Vienna, Austria, completed 1737

Spatial complexity

At the episcopal palace at Bruchsal, Johann Balthasar Neumann was brought in to resolve the architectural difficulties of inserting a new circular stairwell into the existing building. Neumann's understanding of space enabled him to exploit the architectural constraints that had been presented to him to construct a masterpiece of the German Baroque.

Onion dome

The onion dome – a dome that is bulbous at the bottom and tapers to a point at the top – was a consistent feature of Russian and eastern European architecture from the Middle Ages onwards. Baroque architects continued to use it and introduced new variations such as the 'pear' and the 'bud', seen for example in the church of St. Andrew in Kiev, by Francesco Bartolomeo Rastrelli (1700–71).

Johann Balthasar Neumann,
staircase of the Episcopal Palace,
Bruchsal, Germany, 1721–32

Francesco Bartolomeo Rastrelli,
St. Andrew's Church, Kiev,
Ukraine, 1747–54

Region: Spain and Latin America
Period: Seventeenth and eighteenth centuries
Characteristics: Moorish influence; Indigenous American influence; Churrigueresque; Defiance of structure; Dramatic use of light; Heavy mouldings

At the turn of the sixteenth century, a plain and austere classicism, in many ways the architecture of the Renaissance stripped back to its bare essentials of form and geometry, was prevalent in Spain. This style reached its zenith in the work of Juan de Herrera (1530–97), after whom the style – Herrerian – is named. Herrera's most famous work is undoubtedly the great royal palace of San Lorenzo de El Escorial near Madrid for Philip II (r. 1556–98). Herrera inherited the commission when Juan Bautista de Toledo, Philip II's original architect for the project, died in 1567, not long after it began. Herrera modified and enlarged the original plan and reordered the façades to create a near-perfect geometrical synthesis between plan and elevation.

With the spirit of the Counter-Reformation sweeping through the Iberian peninsula, by the mid seventeenth century Baroque features began to augment buildings otherwise characteristic of the Herrerian tradition. However, a uniquely Spanish manifestation of the Baroque began in the work of José Benito de Churriguera (1665–1725), and his brothers Joaquin (1674–1724) and Alberto (1676–1750). They initiated (and lent their name to) the 'Churrigueresque', a dense form of ornamentation that dominated Spanish architecture for much of the eighteenth century. It was used to dramatic effect in Casas y Nóvoa's mid-eighteenth-century west front and towers of the cathedral of Santiago de Compostela, one of Spain's greatest and oldest ecclesiastical buildings.

The Churrigueresque represented a peculiarly Spanish interpretation of the Baroque that was often seen as having been inspired by its Moorish architectural ancestry. Another source was the indigenous architecture of Latin America. After the first Conquistadors landed in the Americas at the end of the fifteenth century, gold flowed back to Spain; the buildings created from these profits in some ways reflected in their architecture the origins of the money that paid for their construction.

A far more certain trend was the spread westwards of the Baroque to the new Spanish dominions across the Atlantic, as much a religious endeavour as an imperial one, if not more so. The great number of Baroque churches that were built in Latin America over the course of the eighteenth century represented the Conquistadors' aim of bringing what they saw as spiritual salvation to Latin America's indigenous population.

Moorish influence

The Moors occupied a large part of the Iberian peninsula from the eighth century CE until the overthrow of the Kingdom of Granada at the end of the fifteenth. The visual similarities have often been noted between the Churrigueresque and Moorish architecture, for example in the Hall of the Abencerrajes in the Alhambra, Granada, which has an extraordinary ceiling articulated by countless *muqarnas* forms.

Hall of the Abencerrajes, Palace of the Lions, Alhambra, Granada, 1354–91

Indigenous American influence

As the Baroque spread into the Americas as the visible expression of Christianity's expanding reach, it proved flexible enough to incorporate elements from the indigenous architecture. Stones from a nearby Inca site, some not even recut, were used in the construction of the Cathedral of Santo Domingo in Cusco, Peru.

Cathedral of Santo Domingo, Cusco, Peru, 1559–1654

Churrigueresque

Named after the Churriguera family, the Churrigueresque style is characterized by the almost complete overloading of a work of architecture with ornamentation. Mouldings, scrolls and foliage – essentially any ornaments deriving from the classical language – were commonly used, but were deployed in the most overwhelming manner. In the Sacristy of the Granada Charterhouse, the sheer density of ornamentation borders on the extreme.

Defiance of structure

At its core, classical architecture is fundamentally an expression of structure. The overwhelming decoration of the Churrigueresque therefore sought to defy this characteristic. In Narciso Tomé's great *El Transparente* altarpiece in Toledo Cathedral, any residual structural expression is overshadowed by the density of ornament; the column shafts appear on the verge of morphing into wholly ornamental features.

Luis de Arévalo and F. Manuel Vasquez, sacristy, Granada Charterhouse, Spain, 1727–64

Narciso Tomé, *El Transparente* altarpiece, Toledo Cathedral, Spain, 1729–32

Dramatic use of light

Another notable feature of the
El Transparente altarpiece, and a key
characteristic of Spanish Baroque, is the
dramatic, almost revelatory use of light.
Tomé removed the non-structural webbing
of the rib vault of the cathedral to allow a
focused beam of light to further heighten
the drama of the altarpiece's extraordinary
ornamentation.

Heavy mouldings

While the Italian Baroque pushed the
boundaries of the accepted use of the
existing repertoire of classical ornament,
the Spanish Baroque developed and
extended the expressive power of the
classical motifs themselves. The Solomonic
(scrolling) column was used frequently,
while even simple mouldings were
dramatically increased in scale to become
expressive architectural features in their
own right.

Narciso Tomé, *El Transparente*
altarpiece, Toledo Cathedral,
Spain, 1729–32

Diego Durán and Cayetano
Sigüenza, Santa Prisca, Taxco,
Mexico, 1751–58

Region: France
Period: Seventeenth to early eighteenth century
Characteristics: Mansard roof; Dome; Landscape design; Licence; Sumptuous interiors; Heavy rustication

The French Baroque is synonymous with the architecture of Louis XIV, King of France (r. 1643–1715). France under Louis was a highly centralized, absolutist state. Power was located in one place – Paris, and later Versailles – and in one person alone – the King – whose actions were regarded as having divine sanction. Louis's esteemed minister, Jean-Baptiste Colbert, directed the arts, and especially architecture, towards the glorification of the self-styled Sun King.

Colbert founded numerous academies, including those for the sciences and for architecture, and undertook a major reorganization of the Académie Royale de Peinture et de Sculpture – all to ensure a steady supply of well-trained artists, architects and engineers to further extend the glory of France. Colbert was instrumental in persuading Bernini to visit Paris in 1665 to prepare designs for the east front of the Louvre. Although these designs were rejected, while in Paris Bernini sculpted a bust of Louis XIV that is regarded as one of the finest representations of the monarch.

Despite Bernini's visit, the Baroque in France developed quite differently from that of southern Europe: firstly in its expression of continuity with the French architectural tradition; and secondly in its close association with palace architecture and landscape design. François Mansart (1598–1666) was the first architect to introduce Baroque styling, principally the frequent use of an applied order and heavy rustication, into the French architectural vocabulary. His church of the Val-de-Grâce in Paris and especially his Château de Maisons, near Paris – with its characteristic mansard roofs – paved the way for the French architects of the following generation.

The château of Vaux-le-Vicomte (1656–61) by Louis Le Vau (1612–70) set the model for the unification of architecture, interior design, painting and landscape design that became the hallmark of the French Baroque. Le Vau's design recalled that of Mansart's Château de Maisons but was more dramatic, with projecting wings, a repeating giant order, and an animated skyline with a central dome and a succession of overlapping mansard roofs. Inside, the painter Charles Le Brun was commissioned to decorate the rooms with sumptuous wall paintings. Outside, André Le Nôtre (1613–1700) extended the architecture of the house into the garden with series of highly ordered, geometrical paths, ponds and hedgerows. Le Vau, Le Brun and Le Nôtre would all be employed by Louis XIV to create his palace of Versailles – arguably the greatest ever built.

Mansard roof

François Mansart did not invent this roof form but it has become associated with him, as he used it frequently. The mansard roof has a practical function in providing more interior space, but for Mansart and subsequent architects its use was emblematic, as it expressed continuity with the French architectural tradition.

François Mansart, Château de Maisons, Maisons-Laffitte, near Paris, 1630–51

Dome

Alongside the palace, the domed church is the pivotal building type of the French Baroque. The best-known example is Jules Hardouin-Mansart's soaring golden dome of St. Louis des Invalides, which stands at the centre of Louis XIV's great hospital for war veterans looking over the River Seine.

Jules Hardouin-Mansart, St. Louis des Invalides, Paris, 1675–1706

Landscape design

At Versailles Le Nôtre's landscape radiated from the palace in a series of long avenues lined with hedges, trees and lawns; a similar arrangement to one that he had earlier employed on a much smaller scale at Vaux-le-Vicomte. Topiary, sculpture and dramatic fountains populated the landscape, representing the physical extension of Louis XIV's dominion.

André Le Nôtre, Orangerie gardens at Château de Versailles, Versailles, from 1661

Licence

In seventeenth-century French philosophy the 'Moderns' argued that the achievements of the present day could equal or even surpass those of antiquity, in stark contrast to the views of the 'Ancients'. In his design for the east front of the Louvre, Paris, the architect–scientist and consummate 'Modern' Claude Perrault (1613–88) rejected received architectural principles to create a façade that was original in composition and architectural expression.

Claude Perrault, east front of the Louvre, Paris, 1665–80

Sumptuous interiors

Louis XIV employed Le Vau, Le Brun and Le Nôtre, and later Hardouin-Mansart, to transform Versailles from a hunting lodge into one of the largest palaces in the world. Its interiors reveal a combination of architecture, gilding and wall painting that creates a visual feast rarely, if ever, surpassed.

Jules Hardouin-Mansart and Charles Le Brun, Hall of Mirrors, Château de Versailles, Versailles, 1678–84

Heavy rustication

The accentuation of the joints between adjacent blocks of masonry – known as rustication – recurred frequently in the French Baroque. This had antecedents in French architecture, notably in the work of the sixteenth-century architect Jacques Androuet du Cerceau (ca. 1520–ca. 1585) and his grandson Salomon de Brosse (ca. 1571–1626), especially the latter's Palais du Luxembourg (begun 1615).

Jules Hardouin-Mansart, Orangerie,
Château de Versailles, Versailles, 1684–6

Region: England
Period: Mid seventeenth to early eighteenth century
Characteristics: Plainness; Animated skyline; Medieval influence; Exaggerated keystones; Eclecticism; Domes

In England the Baroque developed later than and quite differently to how it had done in continental Europe. Protestant England was resistant to the extravagances of the continental Baroque associated with Roman Catholicism, and well into the seventeenth century classical architecture itself was still viewed by some with suspicion. However, links soon developed. On his visit to Paris in 1665, the young Christopher Wren met Bernini himself, an event that proved formative when just a year later the calamity of the Great Fire of London saw that Wren's thoughts turned to rebuilding the capital.

Just days after the Great Fire Wren presented Charles II, King of England (r. 1660–85) with a plan for rebuilding London as a Baroque city of regular, wide boulevards. The pressing need to rebuild immediately and the priorities of private property owners put paid to Wren's scheme. The city was rebuilt on its old medieval plan but its skyline was radically new. The dome of St. Paul's Cathedral and the soaring spires of more than 50 churches – together Wren's defining achievement – heralded London as the first modern city.

A scientist as well as an architect, Wren employed empirical methods to develop highly inventive solutions to architectural problems, for example those inherent in reconciling classical architecture with the medieval spire form. In this Wren was helped by several able assistants, most notably Nicholas Hawksmoor. Working his way up from office clerk to Wren's right-hand man, Hawksmoor was also instrumental in realizing the visions of playwright-turned-architect Sir John Vanbrugh at Castle Howard and Blenheim Palace.

Hawksmoor is, however, best known for the six churches he built across London as part of the 1711 Commission to Build Fifty New Churches. These churches mixed influences ranging from the native Gothic, to Near Eastern and even Egyptian architecture. Christ Church, Spitalfields, with its dramatic west front and curiously Gothic spire, has captured the imagination of generations of Londoners.

However, before Hawksmoor's churches were complete, the Baroque had fallen from fashion. Palladian taste (see page 98), exemplified by the work of Richard Boyle, 3rd Earl of Burlington (1694–1753), came to define English architecture for much of the eighteenth century; Hawksmoor's achievements in particular went unacknowledged and were even ridiculed for their eccentricity and excess.

Plainness

English Baroque architects tended to eschew ornament, and instead relied on the manipulation of light and shade for architectural effect. Hawksmoor's work takes this to the extreme, with some façades reduced to the basic geometrical repetition of arched or circular windows.

Sir John Vanbrugh and Nicholas Hawksmoor, Blenheim Palace, Oxfordshire, 1705–24

Animated skyline

Tightly enclosed by surrounding buildings, the lower parts of Wren's churches were rarely visible, so architectural attention was focused almost solely on the spires. Soon, Vanbrugh, Hawksmoor and Thomas Archer (ca. 1668–1743) began to create animated rooflines for single buildings; Archer's St. John, Smith Square, in particular presents a vivid and unusual silhouette.

Thomas Archer, St. John, Smith Square, London, 1713–28

Medieval influence

In the early eighteenth century medieval architecture was seen as old-fashioned and even morally degenerate. Despite this, used carefully, medieval elements allowed architects to create associations with a distinctly English earlier age. Vanbrugh wrote famously of imparting the 'castle air' at Kimbolton Castle, Cambridgeshire, and even built a faux-medieval castle for himself at Greenwich, London.

Sir John Vanbrugh, Vanbrugh Castle, Greenwich, London, finished 1719

Exaggerated keystones

The most immediately recognizable
characteristic of English Baroque
architecture is the exaggerated keystone.
The first Baroque building in England, the
King Charles block at Greenwich – designed
in the 1660s by Inigo Jones's pupil, John
Webb (1611–72) – makes frequent use of
large keystones, as does the early Baroque
south front at Chatsworth by William
Talman (1650–1719).

William Talman, south front, Chatsworth,
Derbyshire, completed 1696

Eclecticism

English Baroque architects found inspiration in many sources. Despite having never left Britain, Hawksmoor was fascinated by architecture distant in time and place, and elements of early Christian and even Egyptian buildings can be detected in his work. In contrast, James Gibbs (1662–1754) had trained in Rome under the Baroque master Carlo Fontana, whose influence can be seen, for example, in Gibbs's St. Mary le Strand.

Domes

Having seen the then recently constructed domed churches of Paris, even before the Great Fire Wren had wanted to build a dome for old St. Paul's Cathedral to rival that of St. Peter's in Rome. In addition to the new St. Paul's, Wren built three other domed churches in London, the most renowned being the majestic St. Stephen Walbrook.

Nicholas Hawksmoor, St. Mary Woolnoth, London, 1716–24

Sir Christopher Wren, St. Stephen Walbrook, London, 1672–9 (steeple, 1713–17)

Region: Europe, especially France, Germany and Russia
Period: Eighteenth century
Characteristics: *Gesamtkunstwerk*; Continuous spaces; Virtuosity; Asymmetry; Foliate decoration; Secular architecture

The Rococo was the final stage of the Baroque, and in many ways took the Baroque's fundamental qualities of illusion and drama to their logical extremes. In the most complex, multi-layered works of Guarini, for example, the building remains defined by the expression of structure, an idea that went back to the Renaissance. Even the Spanish Churrigueresque (see page 82), the dense ornamentation of which appears to defy architectural structure, actually sought to subsume it, leaving its fundamental architectural and intellectual framework intact.

In contrast to even the late Baroque, Rococo sought to transcend this adherence to structural expression. No longer was ornamentation, however dense, merely augmenting an underlying framework; instead it became the fundamental organizing principle of a space. The purest Rococo spaces were conceived as continuous surfaces – the interplay of light; lustrous, often pastel-coloured materials; and, of course, free-flowing and richly gilded ornamentation pulled the eye in all directions, overwhelming the senses.

Although there are some important Bavarian Rococo churches, such as the wonderful examples at Birnau (1746–9) and Wies (1745–54) that echoed Neumann's pioneering Basilica of the Vierzehnheiligen and, in any case, might actually be regarded as late Baroque, Rococo is most often associated with secular buildings, principally great palaces and salons where educated elites would meet to discuss literary and philosophical ideas. One of the earliest and most famous Rococo creations was the Zwinger Palace in Dresden, Germany, begun in 1711 to the designs of Matthäus Daniel Pöppelmann (1662–1736) for Augustus the Strong, Elector of Saxony (r. 1694–1733). The Zwinger was intended to extend towards the River Elbe and to provide a sumptuous setting for pageants, including a grandstand alongside an orangery. Although it was left incomplete, the lavish architecture, with ornament layered on top of ornament, conjures the appropriate associations of spectacle and fantasy. Arguably the greatest palaces of the Rococo era were designed in Russia by the Italian architect Francesco Bartolomeo Rastrelli, most notably the Winter Palace in St. Petersburg, where Rococo decorative effects enliven the long regal façade.

The Rococo pervaded the entire spectrum of the visual arts. Painters such as Jean-Antoine Watteau and François Boucher often depicted pastoral subjects in soft pastel colours with delicate brushwork, while François de Cuvilliés, Juste-Aurèle Meissonnier, Thomas Chippendale and Thomas Johnson, among others, extended the Rococo's flowing and often sinuous forms into furniture and applied design.

Gesamtkunstwerk

A term usually translated as 'total work of art', the concept of *Gesamtkunstwerk* emerged in nineteenth-century Germany and is particularly associated with the music of the composer Richard Wagner. However, what would later be described as *Gesamtkunstwerk* first appeared in earlier Baroque and especially Rococo architecture, in which interior spaces were treated as syntheses of surface, ornament, furniture, tapestry and painting.

Johann Balthasar Neumann, Spiegelkabinett (Mirror Cabinet), Residenz Würzburg, Bavaria, 1740–45 (rebuilt after World War II)

Continuous spaces

Rococo architects transcended the Baroque insistence on monumental form and therefore spaces defined by the structure. Full of flowing curves, complex geometry and dense ornament, Rococo spaces, such as Johann Michael Fischer's Ottobeuren Abbey in Bavaria, see architectural structure dominated by the exigencies of surface.

Johann Michael Fischer, Ottobeuren Abbey, Bavaria, 1737–66

Virtuosity

Rococo craftsmen achieved a technical virtuosity rarely surpassed before or since. Intricate plaster moulding – often gilded and inset with paintings – finely carved mirror frames and furniture by designers such as Juste-Aurèle Meissonier in France and Thomas Chippendale in England defied comprehension in their skills of craftsmanship, yet in doing so put their makers centre stage.

Nikolaus Pacassi, interior of the Schönbrunn Palace, Vienna, 1743–63

Asymmetry

Rococo designers freed themselves from the adherence to symmetry that had dominated architecture and interior design since the Renaissance. Treating architecture as a fluid plane for embellishment, Rococo designers vastly expanded the existing vocabulary of decorative form, exploiting the excitement of the asymmetrical or the unresolved.

François de Cuvilliés and Johann Balthasar Neumann, Augustusburg Palace, Brühl, Germany, 1700–61

Foliate decoration

Most Rococo decoration consisted of interpretations of various forms of foliage, yet it was quite unlike the superficially similar arabesque or grotesquery. Rendered most often in stucco or wood as part of the building fabric or furniture, Rococo foliage was always twisting and sinuous, with the common serrated-edged raffle leaf form often bordering on the abstract.

François de Cuvilliés, Amalienburg, Nymphenburg Palace, Munich, 1734–9

Secular architecture

As the main cultural manifestation of the spirit of the Counter-Reformation, the Baroque is most often associated with ecclesiastical architecture. The Rococo, on the other hand, was mainly associated with palace and domestic architecture. In Paris, the popularity of the Rococo coincided with the emergence of the salon as a new type of social gathering, the venues for which were often decorated in the Rococo style.

Germain Boffrand and Charles-Joseph Natoire, Salon de la Princesse de Soubise, Hôtel-de-Soubise, Paris, 1735–40

Neoclassicism

In 79 CE the huge volcanic eruption of Vesuvius, which towers over the Gulf of Naples in Italy, buried under a rain of ash the Roman provincial town of Pompeii and the smaller, wealthier resort of nearby Herculaneum. There they remained for centuries, abandoned, buried and forgotten. Parts of Herculaneum were discovered in the sixteenth and seventeenth centuries, only to be reburied. However, in 1738 the Spanish engineer Rocque Joaquin de Alcubierre began the first concerted excavation there after workmen under his direction discovered remains while digging foundations for a palace for the King of Naples. In 1748 Alcubierre discovered Pompeii. As the two Roman towns were gradually uncovered, many visitors came from all over Europe to see the extraordinary range of buildings, complete with surviving frescoes and mosaics, everyday household items and, most poignantly, human remains, all frozen in time.

The discoveries posed fundamental challenges to received opinion on ancient Roman culture. Little sculpture – conventionally seen as the pinnacle of Roman artistic achievement – was found in the excavations. The numerous frescoes were of varying quality and their sometimes sexually explicit content was a surprising revelation to many eighteenth-century sensibilities. Moreover, Alcubierre's excavation methods – which almost encompassed looting – received harsh criticism from the German art historian Johann Joachim Winckelmann especially. Nevertheless, the discovery had a defining impact on Neoclassicism, which reflected the spirit of enquiry and challenge to authority posed by contemporary Enlightenment thought.

The 'Primitive Hut'

As direct, first-hand experience of the Antique, facilitated by the Grand Tour, became an essential part of the education of wealthy young European men, attention was also turning to the origins of ancient architecture. Particularly influential was Abbé Marc-Antoine Laugier's *Essai sur l'architecture* (1753), in which the Jesuit monk put forward the 'primitive hut' as the basis for all 'true' architecture. In many ways recapitulating the Vitruvian precept that architecture was an imitation of nature (see page 52), Laugier argued that classical architecture had evolved from the 'primitive hut': a simple structure of cross-beams supported by tree trunks. Columns, for Laugier, were therefore a 'natural' derivation of the tree trunks. Pilasters, on the other hand, were deemed 'irrational' and a symptom of architecture's debasement from its core principles. Although Laugier's ideas were often fanciful, with little basis in historical fact, they were important in leading the way in a rethinking of architecture from first principles. This conceptual approach was the key innovation of Neoclassicism – in stark contrast to the ornamental imitation of the Antique with which it is often associated.

Into the Nineteenth Century

The Industrial Revolution and the advent of new building technologies and materials in the nineteenth century had diverse effects on Neoclassicism, pushing form and theory in new directions. By focusing on first principles, Neoclassicism could, somewhat counterintuitively, circumvent the conundrum of how to deal with new modern building types. However, that argument depended on the efficacy of those principles, which, once tested, were revealed to be less than universally applicable. It was the German architect and theorist Gottfried Semper (1803–79) who in many ways reconciled Neoclassical principles to the modern age. In his *Die Vier Elemente der Baukunst* (The Four Elements of Architecture; 1851), Semper argued that architecture was a function of recurring elements that were fundamentally shaped by the processes of their creation: weaving, moulding, carpentry, masonry and metalwork. He explained how religious, state and civic institutions – and also industrial ones – created the conditions through which fundamental forms might be given the appropriate architectural expression. Neoclassical principles could therefore be used to make architectural sense of rapid technological change through creating ordered and meaningful forms – in many ways anticipating Modernist Functionalism.

Palladianism

Classical Revival

Greek Revival

Empire Style

Picturesque

Sublime

Region: England and America
Period: Eighteenth century
Characteristics: 'Unity of the whole'; Temple front; 'Natural' landscape gardens; Public buildings; Pattern book architecture; Implied order

In 1715 the architect Colen Campbell (1676–1729) published the first volume of *Vitruvius Britannicus*, the renowned architectural 'manifesto' in which he documented the then current state of architecture in Britain, and attempted to formulate and codify a distinctly British architectural style. Campbell's exemplar was the Mannerist architect Andrea Palladio, most notable for the villas he designed in Italy's Veneto during the mid sixteenth century (see page 68).

Knowledge of Palladio's work had already reached England a century earlier: Inigo Jones had studied Palladio's buildings first-hand in the 1610s and had returned with a number of the great master's drawings. Jones put what he learned from Palladio into practice in several works including the Banqueting House at Whitehall (1619–22) and the Queen's House at Greenwich (begun 1616), both in London. However, the close association of Jones's brand of Palladianism with the courts of James I (r. 1603–25) and his son Charles I (r. 1625–49) saw it fall from favour with the onset of civil war in England. Sir Christopher Wren held Jones in high regard, yet his empirically derived Baroque architecture departed from Jones's work in theory and form. Although works by Wren and also by Sir John Vanbrugh featured in *Vitruvius Britannicus*, Campbell criticized their perceived extravagance, advocating instead the rational ideals exemplified by Palladio and Jones – the purported 'British Vitruvius' of the title.

Campbell's ideas proved influential on Richard Boyle, 3rd Earl of Burlington, who employed the architect ca. 1718 to remodel the façade of his town house in Piccadilly, London. By this time Burlington had visited Italy, and he would do so again to enable him to formulate his own architectural philosophy. Rather than studying Roman buildings directly as he had Palladio's works, Burlington instead relied on the architect's *I quattro libri dell'architettura* (The Four Books of Architecture; 1570), which included systematic surveys of, and abstracted rules from, ancient Roman buildings. Tracing their architectural lineage from the Ancients through their authentic interpreters, Palladio and Jones, Burlington and his aristocratic circle saw themselves as Augustans reborn. Moreover, the architectural style that Burlington and his circle created was codified in concepts of harmony, proportion and virtue – which, it was thought, only those of a 'noble' sensibility could comprehend – to preclude its emulation by those of lower social ranks.

Burlington's Chiswick Villa, London (completed 1729), modelled on Palladio's Villa Rotonda (1566–70), represented the synthesis of his architectural philosophy. After Campbell fell from favour, Burlington turned to William Kent (1685–1748), with whom he forged a successful partnership; so closely were they associated at times that the contemporary critic Horace Walpole described Kent as the 'proper priest' to Burlington as the 'Apollo of the Arts'. Kent, however, was a creative force in his own right, and with other architects was to establish Palladianism as the architectural style of choice among British aristocrats for several decades.

'Unity of the whole'

In his *Essay in Defence of Ancient Architecture* (1728), Palladianism's most eloquent theorist, Robert Morris (ca. 1701/2–54), defined the style in opposition to the 'deformed', 'ridiculous' and 'monstrous' formations of the Gothic and Baroque. He advocated the 'beauty, sweetness and harmony united in the Composition of Ancient Architecture', with all elements acting together to create a 'unity of the whole', illustrated notably by Campbell's Mereworth Castle.

Colen Campbell, Mereworth Castle, Kent, 1720–25

Temple front

Palladio's ideas reached as far as America, where Thomas Jefferson employed a number of Palladian devices, including the temple front in a domestic setting, at Monticello. This was arguably Palladio's most important and influential innovation, the result of his interpretation in *I quattro libri* of the architecture of ancient Rome for modern purposes.

Thomas Jefferson, Monticello, Charlottesville, Virginia, 1769–1809

'Natural' landscape gardens

An undistinguished painter, a good architect but a masterful landscape garden designer, William Kent is an intriguing figure and was far more than Burlington's mere professional proxy. His greatest innovations were in landscape gardening where he extended the 'naturalization' of garden design. His irregular landscapes were punctuated by artfully placed temples, obelisks and statues, recalling the Italian gardens, ancient and modern, he had himself seen.

William Kent, garden at Rousham, Oxfordshire, 1738–41

Public buildings

The emergence of the modern political state at the end of the seventeenth century required new building types to express its functions. As Palladio had designed not only villas, but town palaces, churches and even a theatre, his architectural language, as expressed in *I quattro libri*, could be readily adapted, for example in Horse Guards, which accommodated barracks and the offices of the Secretary of War.

William Kent and John Vardy, Horse Guards, London, 1751–8

Pattern book architecture

Giacomo Leoni's translation (1716–20) of *I quattro libri* popularized Palladio's ideas in Britain. Some builders, however, treated it more as a pattern book than an architectural treatise. The poet Alexander Pope satirized the way in which fashionable Palladian windows were often deployed with little understanding of their meaning or function. Despite his deep knowledge of Palladio's architecture, Leoni often fused Baroque and Palladian styles in his own work.

Giacomo Leoni, Clandon Park, Surrey, 1730–33

Implied order

In an urban context it was not just grand town palaces and public buildings that were informed by Palladian ideals. An 'implied order' – the arrangement of windows and cornices in a way that suggested an underlying order without the need for classical ornamentation – imbued even relatively undistinguished town houses with Palladianism's latent moral qualities, countering concerns about speculative development and urban expansion.

John Wood the Younger, Royal Crescent, Bath, 1767–71

Region: Europe and America
Period: Mid eighteenth to mid nineteenth century
Characteristics: Roman ornament; Quotation; Columns; Archetypal forms; Arches; City grid

To suggest that a Classical Revival began in Europe about 1750 seems counterintuitive. Since the Renaissance, classicism had been firmly entrenched as the dominant mode of architectural expression. Palladianism was a reaction to the perceived extravagance and licence of the Baroque, and sought to reaffirm architecture's link to the Ancients, as mediated by Palladio. However, by the 1750s architects inspired by their experiences on the Grand Tour, and perhaps also by Abbé Laugier's writings on the origins of classical architecture, began to seek direct inspiration from the remains of the architecture of antiquity.

One of the central figures of the Classical Revival was the Scottish architect Robert Adam (1728–92). Even though his father, William Adam (1689–1748), was Scotland's leading architect, Robert recognized the advantage of first-hand experience of Roman antiquities. In 1754 he set off for Italy on the well-trodden route of the Grand Tour. He toured the country before settling for a time in Rome, where he met the French draughtsman Charles-Louis Clérisseau (1721–1820) and the renowned Italian artist Giovanni Battista Piranesi (1720–78). Under their tutelage Adam refined his drawing technique, and began to forge an understanding of the Antique as something that was fluid and evolving and which presented plentiful opportunities for architectural appropriation. Before returning to London, he undertook a five-week-long expedition, accompanied by Clérisseau, to the ruins of the Roman emperor Diocletian's palace at Spalato (present-day Split) on the Dalmatian coast. There, Adam, Clérisseau and a team of four Italians conducted detailed surveys of the ruins from which they produced a number of topographical views and *capricci*, imagined views of the site in the time of Diocletian (r. 284–305 CE).

Shortly after his return Adam published *Ruins of the Palace of the Emperor Diocletian at Spalatro in Dalmatia* (1764), which established his reputation and became a frequent source for his famous 'Adam Style' interiors combining colourful and highly ornate Neoclassical ornament with sumptuous craftsmanship. Having gone into business with his brother James (1732–94), for the next two decades Adam became Britain's most sought-after architect. He was also appointed joint architect of the King's Works alongside his old rival, Sir William Chambers (1723–96), who had also visited Italy during the late 1750s.

Although the fashion for 'Adam Style' interiors passed relatively quickly, the Classical Revival evolved in new directions, informed by the ideas of the French theorist Quatremère de Quincy (1755–1849) and the German architect Gottfried Semper, whose notion of recurring archetypal forms helped to reconcile Neoclassicism to modernity. On an urban scale, the gridded plan for the new American capital of Washington, DC, drawn up in 1791 by Pierre Charles L'Enfant (1754–1825), fused the regularity of ancient Roman city plans with a rational underpinning characteristic of the Enlightenment.

Roman ornament

Robert Adam was arguably the first architect to integrate the fireplaces, furniture, carpets and other furnishings of a room into a unified decorative scheme. With his brother James, Adam employed a team of craftsmen to realize the complex designs of grotesque, arabesque and other Neoclassical motifs, which, in contrast to those of the Rococo, appealed to the intellect as much as to the senses.

Quotation

Following the Palladian architects who had begun the house, Adam used a number of intriguing Neoclassical quotations in his work at Kedleston Hall. The centrepiece of the great south front, a blind triumphal arch, is closely inspired by the Arch of Constantine in Rome (see page 15), the coffered dome of its interior references the Pantheon (see page 14), while its columned hall recalled the atrium of a Roman villa.

Robert Adam, Long Gallery,
Syon House, Middlesex,
England, 1762

Robert Adam, south front,
Kedleston Hall, Derbyshire,
England, 1760–70

Columns

A follower of Abbé Laugier, Jacques-Germaine Soufflot (1713–80) made a remarkable innovation in the church dedicated to Ste. Genevieve (now the Panthéon) that he designed: he used freestanding columns to create an ambulatory along the whole perimeter of its Greek cross plan. This use of columns rather than walls or pilasters followed Laugier's theories of the 'primitive hut'.

Jacques-Germaine Soufflot, Panthéon (formerly Ste. Genevieve), Paris, 1755–92

Archetypal forms

Semper's opera house in Dresden is actually the second that he built on the site, the first having burned down in 1869. Both designs appear influenced by the overtly Neoclassical theatre designed by Friedrich Gilly (1772–1800) in the 1790s (unbuilt); however, Semper goes further, composing a series of volumes that make clear the internal spatial configurations informed by the musical and theatrical innovations of his friend Richard Wagner, the composer.

Gottfried Semper, Semperoper, Dresden, Germany, 1871–8

Arches

The archetypal component of Roman architecture, and arguably its greatest innovation (see page 12), the arch was a key feature of the Classical Revival, where it was often deployed in monumental arcades. Chambers set the long façade of Somerset House above a tall arcade, which the Thames flowed into before its embankment in the nineteenth century. This arcade was a grander version of the one his rival, Robert Adam, had designed upstream at the Adelphi.

Sir William Chambers, Somerset House, London, 1776–1801

City grid

In 1791, L'Enfant was asked by the first
President of the United States, George
Washington, to draw up a plan for a
new capital city on the Potomac River.
L'Enfant specified the locations for the
present Capitol Building and White House,
thereby inscribing in space the governance
structure inscribed in the new country's
constitution. In conceiving this important
plan, L'Enfant combined ancient Roman
precedent with Enlightenment rationality.

Aerial view of Capitol Building and
Washington, DC, planned by Pierre Charles
L'Enfant with revisions by Andrew Ellicott,
begun 1791

Region: Europe, especially England and Germany
Period: Mid eighteenth to mid nineteenth century
Characteristics: Polychromy; Archaeological accuracy; Greek Doric order; Interpretation; Quotation; Commodification of antiquity

While Italy, the prime destination for Grand Tourists, contained some important ancient Greek ruins, notably the colony at Paestum, recorded so vividly by Piranesi, Greece itself was much further afield and, during the eighteenth century, still part of the Ottoman Empire. So when the two Englishmen James 'Athenian' Stuart (1713–88) and Nicholas Revett (1720–1804) decided in 1748 to venture to Greece, (though they did not start their journey until 1751), they were stepping beyond the usual well-trodden path of the Grand Tour, exploring the relatively unknown; indeed, the spectre of plague actually hastened their return in 1754. In the intervening years they carefully surveyed the ancient remains that they discovered; Revett took detailed measurements and recordings that Stuart then used for the trigonometric reconstructions of his topographical views, which he produced alongside written accounts.

Several years after their return to England, Stuart and Revett published the first volume of *The Antiquities of Athens* (1762), followed quickly by two more. In its preface Stuart asserted the primacy of Greek culture over Roman, and of Athens in particular: 'Greece is the Place where the most beautiful Edifices were erected and where the purest and most elegant Examples of ancient Architecture are to be discovered.' For a work intended in part to advertise its authors' rare and specialist knowledge of Greek antiquities to potential clients, this was an obvious claim to make, yet it also reflected the emerging contemporary belief that Greece was the birthplace of Western civilization.

One of the principle figures in establishing and promoting interest in Greek culture was the German art historian Johann Joachim Winckelmann. From an early age Winckelmann had immersed himself in Greek literature and art. In the 1750s he moved to Rome to study its antiquities at first hand. His skills of observation and analysis led him to conclude that many of the works and ideas of Roman art history were actually Greek in origin. Partly for that reason he identified Greek culture as the true model for imitation and emulation in his magnum opus, *Geschichte der Kunst des Alterthums* (The History of the Art of Antiquity), of 1764.

Winckelmann's work was influential all over Europe but was particularly important in Germany, not only for the following generation of scholars and writers such as Immanuel Kant and Johann Wolfgang von Goethe, but for architecture too, and notably his fellow Prussian Karl Friedrich Schinkel (1781–1841). Under the patronage of Frederick William III, King of Prussia (r. 1797–1840), and his son the Crown Prince, later Frederick William IV (r. 1840–61), Schinkel realized several important buildings in Berlin that were designed to align symbolically the Prussian state with the ideals of fifth-century Athens. His Schauspielhaus (1818–21), Altes Museum (1823–30) and Bauakademie (1832–6) put into practice his contention that 'if one could preserve the spiritual principle of Greek architecture, [and] bring it to terms with the conditions of our own epoch … then one could find the most genuine answer to our discussion'.

Polychromy

Winckelmann believed that classical sculpture had originally been white, and promoted the idea that the purer the white the more beautiful the form. Quatremère-de-Quincy, in his *Le Jupiter Olympien* (1814), was among the first to recognize that Greek sculpture had been polychromatic. Yet the intense colour of decorative architectural effects, notably those by 'Athenian' Stuart, suggests that polychromy was already assumed to be integral to Greek culture.

James 'Athenian' Stuart, Painted Room, Spencer House, London, 1759–65

Archaeological accuracy

The Greek Revival style was the logical choice for the British Museum, which purported to document the history of Western culture. Sir Robert Smirke (1780–1867) employed the Ionic order of the Erechtheion on the Acropolis in Athens (one of its original caryatids was actually in the museum's collection) in his design. The accuracy of his quotation from ancient architecture reflected the spirit of rational observation that characterized this epochal Enlightenment project.

Sir Robert Smirke, British Museum, London, 1823–52

Greek Doric order

Renaissance theorists had largely ignored the Greek Doric in favour of the Roman version of the order, which was similar to the Tuscan in its heaviness and simple mouldings. Increasingly prevalent towards the end of the eighteenth century, the Greek Doric was characterized by plain flared capitals and fluted columns without bases. These supported an entablature of metopes and triglyphs, a characteristic shared with the Roman Doric.

William Wilkins, The Grange, Northington, Hampshire, England, 1804–9

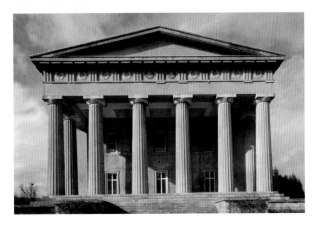

Interpretation

While he was deeply inspired by Greek architecture and frequently used forms derived from it, Schinkel opposed the slavish imitation of antiquity. He argued that while the ancient Greek was an appropriate model, 'each work of art, of whatever kind, must always contain a new element, and be a living addition to the world of art' – illustrated in his Greek-inspired yet decidedly contemporary Altes Museum.

Karl Friedrich Schinkel, Altes Museum, Berlin, 1823–30

Quotation

It was not just individual elements that were appropriated in Greek Revival architecture, but whole buildings or structures. Hamilton's monument to the great Scottish poet Robert Burns, on Calton Hill in Edinburgh, was a faithful yet slightly enlarged version of the Choragic Monument of Lysicrates in Athens (see page 9).

Commodification of antiquity

The fashion for all things Greek presented huge commercial opportunities not just for architects but for designers of all specialisms. One of the most successful was the English potter Josiah Wedgwood, whose renowned 'Jasperware' re-created the forms and appearance of antique pottery and could be produced on a near-industrial scale, to be marketed and sold widely.

Thomas Hamilton, Burns Monument, Edinburgh, 1820–31

Assorted Wedgwood 'Jasperware', produced in England, late eighteenth century

Region: France
Period: Late eighteenth to mid nineteenth century
Characteristics: Corinthian order; Monumentality; Spoliation; Imperial symbolism; Severity; Interiors

The rise of the public sphere and, more broadly, the spread of Enlightenment thought in the eighteenth century posed fundamental questions for Church and state. In France Enlightenment philosophers and theorists both reflected and exploited increasing dissatisfaction with an overbearing Catholic Church and the absolutist Bourbon monarchy. In his most influential work, *Du contract social ou principes du droit politique* (The Social Contract; 1762), the great Genevan philosopher Jean-Jacques Rousseau advocated a civil society in which religious tolerance and democracy flourished and sovereignty was inscribed in the rule of law. The rights of the individual, trammelled under absolutism, would be secured through submission to the general will of the people, in which the individual, as one of the people, had an obvious stake – the essence of the social contract.

The model of the Roman Republic was increasingly idealized in both philosophical and political discourse as well as in art. The great Neoclassical painter Jacques-Louis David's *Oath of the Horatii* (1784) reflected the spirit of heroic self-sacrifice inspired by the republican ideal. Behind the dynamic tripartite arrangement of the figures, three barely ornamented Doric arches frame the scene. Providing a distinct contrast to the frippery of the Rococo, their stark severity serves to heighten the drama unfolding before them. This preference for austere Roman Neoclassicism pervaded all areas of the decorative arts, including furniture design and fashion, both before and after the French Revolution. It also informed the extraordinary festivals dedicated to the celebration of 'Reason' and the 'Supreme Being' that David

organized for the propaganda purposes of his friend the politician Maximilien Robespierre, under whose leadership the extreme violence known as the Reign of Terror (1793–4) had swept through France.

In this turbulent climate little new architecture was built (although Notre Dame, Paris, and other ecclesiastical buildings were co-opted as 'Temples of Reason'). It was only with the rise of Napoleon that architecture began to figure centrally in grand acts of political and personal ceremony. After much political manoeuvring, Napoleon Bonaparte had in a few short years gone from artillery commander to general, consul and eventually emperor, crowning himself in Notre Dame in the presence of Pope Pius VII in 1804. A genius of military strategy, Napoleon recognized the importance of commemorating his victories, especially the Battle of Austerlitz (1805), in monumental architecture as a way of bolstering and furthering his power. While the pre- and post-Revolutionary periods looked to republican Rome, Napoleon and his architects, notably the duo of Charles Percier (1764–1838) and Pierre-François-Léonard Fontaine (1762–1853), were inspired by the forms and iconography of imperial Rome. Triumphal arches and columns were the most obvious manifestations of a highly symbolic, sometimes bombastic, form of Neoclassicism. While often heavy with imposing ornament, Percier and Fontaine's work in and around Paris, at the Louvre, the Palais des Tuileries and the Château de Malmaison, constituted a fusion of Enlightenment-influenced principles of rationality with imperial iconography, creating an architecture of enduring resonance.

Corinthian order

In contrast to the Doric severity seen in David's paintings, and the austere Neoclassicism of the pre- and post-Revolutionary period, Napoleon's Empire Style made frequent use of the ornate Corinthian order. By adding a twelve-columned Corinthian portico to the Palais Bourbon, Bernard Poyet (1742–1824) created a monumental façade looking across the River Seine towards the Place de la Concorde and La Madeleine beyond.

Bernard Poyet, portico, Palais Bourbon (now Assemblée Nationale), Paris, 1806–8

Monumentality

After much wrangling Pierre-Alexandre Vignon (1762–1828) was personally commissioned by Napoleon to design a temple to the glories of his Grande Armée. Vignon erected a monumental octastyle peripteral temple with 52 columns, 20 metres (60 feet) high, inspired by the Maison Carrée, a wonderfully preserved Roman temple at Nîmes (see page 13). Before the building was complete, however, the decision was taken to turn it into a church, known as La Madeleine.

Pierre-Alexandre Vignon, La Madeleine, Paris, 1807–42

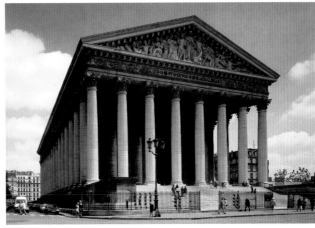

Spoliation

Percier and Fontaine's Arc de Triomphe de Carrousel, which stood between the Louvre and the Palais des Tuileries before the latter's destruction, was based on the Arch of Constantine in Rome (see page 15). Bas reliefs depicted Napoleon's victories while sculptures of horses, looted from St. Mark's Basilica in Venice, originally crowned the monument. Before it was finished, an even larger Arc de Triomphe was commissioned from Jean Chalgrin (1739–1811).

Charles Percier and Pierre-François-Léonard Fontaine, Arc de Triomphe de Carrousel, Paris, 1806–8

Imperial symbolism

The Empire Style was infused with and dominated by symbolic motifs, including eagles, wreaths and even the letter N (for Napoleon). Based on Trajan's Column, the bronze reliefs designed by Pierre-Nolasque Bergeret, a pupil of David, for the column in the Place Vendôme commemorated Napoleon's victory at Austerlitz. Atop it was a version of Antonio Canova's *Napoleon as Mars the Peacemaker* (1802–6) by Antoine-Denis Chaudet.

Jacques Gondouin and Jean-Baptiste Lepère, Vendôme Column, Paris, 1806–10

Severity

David's paintings during the 1780s, which also included the *Death of Socrates* (1787) and *The Lictors Bring to Brutus the Bodies of His Sons* (1789) – the latter exhibited when the Revolution had already begun – promoted the idea of heroic male self-sacrifice. The high drama of the scenes is amplified by their severe Neoclassical settings, linking architecture with political and individual action.

Jacques-Louis David, *Oath of the Horatii*, oil on canvas, 1784

Interiors

The Neoclassical influence extended to the architecture of interiors. The interiors of Napoleon's Château de Malmaison, where the Empress Josephine commissioned Percier and Fontaine to make numerous and expensive alterations, had a loosely martial theme. A tent motif was used in several bedchambers, including that of the Empress, which incorporated a bed by François-Honoré-Georges Jacob-Desmalter, one of the greatest furniture makers of the period.

François-Honoré-Georges Jacob-Desmalter, The Bed of the Empress, Château de Malmaison, Rueil-Malmaison, France, 1810

Region: Europe, especially England and France
Period: Late eighteenth to early nineteenth century
Characteristics: Asymmetry; Sham ruins; Painterly; Rustic; Exotic; Picturesque urbanism

Picturesque literally means 'like a picture', and more specifically, in derivation from the Italian *pittoresco*, 'like a painting'. This definition shaped the way the term was co-opted to represent a particular aesthetic ideal in the cultural debates of the mid to late eighteenth century. The idealized classical landscapes of seventeenth-century painters such as Nicolas Poussin, Claude Lorrain and Salvator Rosa had long been held in high regard, in Britain especially, and had proved influential on landscape gardening. However, it was arguably Edmund Burke's theory of the Sublime, the antithesis of the notion of the Beautiful, that precipitated the emergence of the Picturesque as a coherent aesthetic category.

The Beautiful derived from classical principles of formal harmony and proportion as well as material qualities, although debates raged as to the extent to which beauty was innate or acquired. Joseph Addison, writing in *The Spectator* in 1712, popularized the notion of primary and secondary 'pleasures of the imagination'; the first derived from what the eye sees before it, and the second from memory and the assimilation of past experiences. The Sublime, in contrast, was the raw, visceral sensation of being psychologically and even physically overwhelmed by the experience of a towering mountain, a sweeping canyon or even a work of architecture. In his *Essay on the Picturesque* (1794), Uvedale Price (1747–1829), one of the Picturesque's foremost theorists, argued that a painterly composition of formal contrasts and similarities, and differing scales and associations, sitting between the poles of the Beautiful and the Sublime, best induced aesthetic pleasure.

It was Price's fellow English theorist Richard Payne Knight (1750–1824) who arguably first put Picturesque principles into practice at his Herefordshire house, Downton Castle (1772–8). Claiming to be directly inspired by a painting by Lorrain, Knight designed an asymmetrical house in a Gothic idiom (albeit with Neoclassical interiors) that was intended to conjure Picturesque views from every angle. Knight's use of the Gothic reflected the way in which the Enlightenment spirit of enquiry had investigated not only classical antiquity but Britain's native Gothic heritage too. This tendency was also seen in the increase in domestic tourism towards the end of the eighteenth century, especially to ruined abbeys such as Fountains and Rievaulx in Yorkshire and Tintern in Monmouthshire, the latter famously painted by J.M.W. Turner.

Landscape gardening was, however, the field in which Picturesque ideas undoubtedly had their greatest influence, notably in the work of the prolific Humphry Repton (1752–1818). Following the death of Lancelot 'Capability' Brown (1716–83), Repton assumed the mantle of Britain's leading landscape designer. In contrast to the huge earthworks often required by Brown's designs, Repton tended to augment or 'improve' existing landscapes with artfully placed groups of trees and architectural eye-catchers. Repton frequently used his skills as a watercolourist to create evocative 'before' and 'after' views in his famous 'Red Books', which both conveyed the painterly composition of his designs and advertised his talents to patrons.

Asymmetry

Many designers revelled in the Picturesque
possibilities of asymmetry as an antidote
to the formal rigidities of classical design.
However, it was not just Gothic structures
that played with asymmetry; John Nash's
Cronkhill, designed for Thomas Noel Hill,
2nd Baron Berwick, who lived nearby at
Attingham Park, was an extraordinarily
free interpretation of an Italian villa, with
a loggia, wide, overhanging eaves and
a tower with a cone-shaped roof.

John Nash, Cronkhill, Shropshire,
England, 1802–5

Sham ruins

George Lyttelton, 1st Baron Lyttelton, a politician and close associate of Frederick, Prince of Wales, employed Sanderson Miller (1716–80) to design a mock ruined castle in the grounds of Hagley Hall. Miller's design was based on a plan with four corner towers, only one of which was completed; the others appeared to be 'ruined' but were linked by a wall with its windows left open to create an evocative Picturesque silhouette.

Sanderson Miller, mock castle, Hagley Hall, Worcestershire, England, begun 1747

Painterly

Repton's 'Red Books' were important in showing how his designs were composed like paintings. At Kenwood House, for example, he disrupted the parkland's wide views with artfully placed groups of trees and paths that led viewers around the garden to particular spots where its full Picturesque effect would be revealed. The sham bridge at Kenwood probably predates Repton's work but became integral to his composition.

Humphry Repton, Kenwood House, Hampstead, London, 1786 (rebuilt 1791)

Rustic

Marie-Antoinette, Queen of France, was given the Petit Trianon by her husband, Louis XVI, after his accession to the throne. She commissioned Richard Mique (1728–94) to design a Picturesque hamlet in its gardens, complete with farmhouse and working dairy, to act as a rustic retreat from the intrigues of the palace of Versailles. Mique made use of various vernacular styles in designing the village, which has become the best-known example of the popular Picturesque 'Cottage Style'.

Richard Mique, Hameau de la Reine (The Queen's Hamlet), near the Petit Trianon, Versailles, 1783

Exotic

It was not only native medieval heritage that Neoclassicism had helped popularize, but the architecture of distant places too. As the taste for Chinese design swept Europe, Gustav III, King of Sweden (r. 1771–92), commissioned an elegant and sumptuously decorated Chinese Pavilion for the grounds of his palace at Drottningholm. Picturesque theory provided a philosophical underpinning for these acts of appropriation, which had begun to occur from the mid eighteenth century.

Carl Johan Cronstedt and Carl Fredrik Adelcrantz, Chinese Pavilion, Drottningholm Palace, Lovön, Sweden, 1760

Picturesque urbanism

In 1811 John Nash (1752–1835) was commissioned by the Prince Regent (later George IV, King of England; r. 1820–30) to produce a masterplan for what would become Regent's Park and its surrounding area in London. Nash's design included grand stuccoed terraces and villas arranged in elegant set-backs and crescents, which he integrated with other commissions for the prince including Regent Street, Carlton House Terrace, Marble Arch and Buckingham Palace.

John Nash, Park Square and Park Crescent, London, 1819–24

Region: Europe, especially England and France
Period: Late eighteenth to mid nineteenth century
Characteristics: Ancient Sublime; Visionary Sublime; Formal Sublime; Industrial Sublime; Technical Sublime; Ethereal Sublime

The notion of the Sublime is inextricably linked with the experience of the Grand Tour. Crossing the Alps and encountering landscapes on a scale that they could scarcely have imagined, the Grand Tourists would have been astonished by the range of antiquities they saw when they finally reached Italy, from colossal temples and acres of ruins to exalted works of classical sculpture. While prints depicting the monuments of the Ancients were in wide circulation, few conveyed their sheer majesty. One artist who was able to do so was Giovanni Battista Piranesi, whose atmospheric engravings rendered Roman antiquities as curiously otherworldly. His famous *Carceri* (Prisons; begun 1745) etchings of semi-fictitious labyrinthine vaults, populated by faceless prisoners operating vast machines, were inspired by, and accentuated the profound psychological effect of, encountering the Antique.

These types of experience were important in informing Edmund Burke's theory of the Sublime, articulated in an influential essay of 1757. While, for Burke, the Beautiful resided in what was orderly and structured, the Sublime was the deeply-felt sensation of terror – ultimately of fear – induced by an overpowering aesthetic experience, arguably most profoundly of nature, but also of architecture. Burke's concept was highly influential on aesthetic theory, and was developed – and critiqued – by both Kant and Arthur Schopenhauer. In English architecture, its indirect impact can be seen in the work of George Dance the Younger (1741–1825) and his pupil, Sir John Soane (1753–1837). Dance had

met Piranesi while in Rome, and several of his major works, such as Newgate Prison (1769–77) and St. Luke's Hospital for the Insane (1780) in London, both now demolished, reveal the Italian's influence. The austere façades of these two buildings alluded to the disturbing life of their interiors. Soane's work, while often similarly barely ornamented, was remarkable for its use of light. At the Bank of England and on a smaller scale in his own house in Lincoln's Inn Fields, both in London, he made dramatic use of pendentive domes – a favourite device – to manipulate light in such a way that it becomes the very essence of architecture.

In France the Sublime is most closely associated with the work of Étienne-Louis Boullée (1728–99) and Claude-Nicolas Ledoux (1736–1806). Boullée built relatively few buildings, with even fewer examples still surviving, but is best remembered for his fantastical architectural visions of the 1780s and 1790s. Stripping architecture back to its bare geometric forms, his designs, such as the Cenotaph for Isaac Newton, are among the most megalomaniacal ever produced. Ledoux was arguably no less ambitious in his aspirations, though he built more and favoured raw abstract forms over direct imitation of the Ancients. Boullée and Ledoux proved influential on Jean-Nicolas-Louis Durand (1760–1834), who as professor of architecture at the École Polytechnique popularized the idea of architecture as a rational construct of modular components, in many ways prefiguring the standardization of later centuries.

Ancient Sublime

Piranesi's *Carceri* etchings are at root
capricci: imaginary views of assembled
architectural subjects. However, his
theatrical accentuation of ancient
architectural forms with dramatic light
and shade, and their relatively large scale,
give them an eerie, otherworldly feel. The
etchings influenced the work of a number
of architects as well as writers such
as Samuel Taylor Coleridge and Edgar
Allan Poe.

Giovanni Battista Piranesi, *Carceri*, VII,
etching, 1760

Visionary Sublime

Boullée's unbuilt cenotaph for the
seventeenth-century English scientist
Sir Isaac Newton is the best-known
example of his visionary architecture. The
megalomaniacal – and wholly unbuildable –
design, which envisioned a 150-metre-wide
(492-foot-wide) sphere resting on a round
base, ringed with cypress trees, reflected
both Boullée's Neoclassical interests and
his response, in form and geometry, to the
fundamental laws of physics that Newton
had identified.

Étienne-Louis Boullée, section at night,
Cenotaph for Isaac Newton (unbuilt), 1784

Formal Sublime

After the Royal Saltworks at Arc-et-Senans, Ledoux's most significant works were what he described as 'Les Propylées de Paris', gateways to Paris that were also barriers, erected to collect duties and dissuade smuggling, which were modelled on the monumental Propylaea entrances to the Acropolis in Athens. The unadorned masonry and stark repetition of forms conjure a feeling of grand scale even if the buildings themselves are not particularly large.

Claude-Nicolas Ledoux, Barrière de la Villette, Paris, 1785–9

Industrial Sublime

The two colossal arches of Lewis Cubitt's King's Cross Station border on Functionalism in their direct relationship to the twin train sheds lying behind them. Yet their sheer overpowering scale also conveys the spirit and ambition of Victorian engineering (in stark contrast to the Gothic confection of George Gilbert Scott's adjacent Midland Hotel, see page 127), and illustrates how the Sublime could give meaning to new industrial building types.

Lewis Cubitt, King's Cross Station, London, 1851–2

Technical Sublime

As chief engineer for the Great Western Railway, Isambard Kingdom Brunel (1806–59) was charged with laying the route from London's Paddington Station (the soaring train sheds of which he later designed) to Bristol and Exeter. His extraordinary suspension bridge crossing high above the River Avon in Bristol still elicits fear and wonderment in near equal measure, and remains a symbolic representation of the march of technological progress.

Isambard Kingdom Brunel, Clifton Suspension Bridge, Bristol, England, designed 1829–31, constructed 1836–64

Ethereal Sublime

Sir John Soane rebuilt three houses
along the north side of Lincoln's Inns
Fields in stages between 1792 and 1824.
Together, they served as home, office and
'museum' for his extraordinary collection of
antiquities, while the buildings themselves
were a demonstration of his architectural
ideas. Soane's famous Breakfast Room is a
coherent exposition of his interest in light,
over and above material form, as the very
essence of architecture.

Sir John Soane, Breakfast Room, Sir John
Soane's Museum, Lincoln's Inn Fields, London,
1808–13

Eclecticism

Since the Renaissance architects had essentially followed the Vitruvian precept that architecture was an imitation of nature. The advent of the Industrial Revolution, which began in England towards the end of the eighteenth century, had a complex and significant impact on that assumption, and almost every other about architecture. Before the Industrial Revolution patronage for architects had been confined almost exclusively to the state, the Church and the aristocracy. Economic and social changes saw a new class of patrons emerge – the bourgeoisie – who were wealthy company owners and industrialists with the capital and inclination to build on a grand scale. New ways of organizing and dividing labour and other transformations in society inaugurated new building types: not only the factory and the warehouse, but also the hospital, prison, bank, municipal library, town hall and railway station. New materials and advances in engineering, notably in the use of iron and plate glass, presented new structural opportunities for architects but also problems in reconciling these materials to existing architectural languages. It was no surprise that it was engineers rather than architects who were the first to exploit the possibilities of iron and, later, steel: a development that marked a decisive break between the two disciplines.

Stylistic Relativism

The upheavals in terms of patronage, new building types and new materials inaugurated by the Industrial Revolution irrevocably eroded the dominance of Renaissance principles and, ultimately, those of classical antiquity in governing architectural theory and practice. Without this single overarching authority stylistic relativism ensued, and styles outside the classical canon – some even beyond the Western tradition – assumed currency and legitimacy. Eclecticism, therefore, describes an architectural culture in which the Gothic Revival could co-exist with Beaux-Arts academic classicism, and where imperialist Orientalism would lead to the proliferation of styles as diverse as Chinese, Indian, Egyptian, Moorish and Mayan.

Ruskin and Morris

Despite the comparative stylistic freedom granted to architects, a prevalent and significant school of thought, led by the Englishmen John Ruskin (1819–1900) and later William Morris (1834–96), was suspicious of the effect of the new social, economic and material conditions of modernity on traditional craftsmanship. Ruskin reacted strongly to the encroachments of mechanization and standardization in architectural production. His essay *The Seven Lamps of Architecture* (1849) codified his theory of architecture as the direct expression of its craftsman, through whose honest workmanship and fidelity to the qualities of materials a transcendent beauty might be attained. Ruskin's predisposition was to the Gothic and he followed many of the earlier ideas of the Gothic Revivalist A.W.N. Pugin (1812–52), who had sought, through architecture, a return to the aesthetic and moral realities of the Middle Ages. Ruskin's advocacy of traditional aesthetic values and craftsmanship was largely taken up by William Morris, whose Arts and Crafts movement aimed at integrating aesthetic and social reform.

Structural Rationalism

While Pugin, Ruskin and Morris were, despite their differences, essentially anti-modern in their reaction to the social, aesthetic and religious upheavals that modernity had initiated, other thinkers, notably the French architect Eugène-Emmanuel Viollet-le-Duc (1814–79), saw more obvious potential in modern materials. Although he also resorted to the Gothic, his reasons for doing so were considerably different, as he regarded medieval Gothic architecture as the uniquely rational expression of the structural possibilities of stone and brick. Viollet-le-Duc argued that this same rational approach should be applied when dealing with iron and plate glass, the materials of the new industrial age. Putting his theory into practice proved rather more difficult, and Viollet-le-Duc is better remembered for his creative restoration of numerous medieval structures across France (in distinct contrast to the non-interventionist approach advocated by Ruskin).

Gothic Revival

Orientalism

Beaux-Arts

Arts and Crafts

Art Nouveau

Art Deco

Region: Europe, especially England; also the United States and Canada
Period: Nineteenth century
Characteristics: Restitutive Gothic; Structural Gothic; Natural Gothic; Eclectic Gothic; Ruskinian Gothic; Modern Gothic

Since the time of the Renaissance, Gothic architecture had been broadly perceived as ugly, irrational, unsound – the dangerous 'Other' of the purity of classicism. Giorgio Vasari's mid-sixteenth-century argument that the barbarian hordes of the 'Goths' and 'Visigoths' had not only destroyed Roman architecture in the fifth and sixth centuries CE, but civilization itself, had lasting currency (see page 66). Early attempts to combine classical architecture with Gothic elements, for example in the work of Nicholas Hawksmoor and Sir John Vanbrugh in England, had had little influence. Horace Walpole's fantastical 'Gothick' villa, Strawberry Hill in Twickenham, Middlesex (1749–76), exemplified the sensibility that valued the Gothic for its Picturesque associations but that had little interest in archaeological fidelity or the meaning Gothic architecture might have held in the Middle Ages.

By the 1830s the arguments of the High Anglican Oxford Movement for a return to lost medieval religious traditions had attained prominence, a tendency that eventually morphed into Anglo-Catholicism. Architecturally this was best exemplified in the work of the prolific architect and theorist A.W.N. Pugin (who himself became a Catholic in 1834). Pugin argued that an authentically medieval Gothic style of architecture would facilitate a return to a morally virtuous medieval faith and society. As evidence for this, his book *Contrasts* (1836) juxtaposed fifteenth-century buildings with contemporary ones; the stark differences between the benign charity provided by a medieval monastery and the harsh conditions of a nineteenth-century workhouse were, for Pugin, obvious in their implications.

Although largely disparaging of Pugin, John Ruskin appeared to owe many of his ideas to Pugin's example. *The Stones of Venice* (1853) was arguably Ruskin's most coherent statement of his architectural theory expanding his earlier *Seven Lamps of Architecture*. In these works Ruskin rejected the classical tradition, seeing it as pagan in derivation and stupefied in revival, all the while making slaves of its workmen. The Gothic, he argued, was contrastingly natural and fluid, and allowed craftsmen opportunity for individual expression. For Ruskin the Gothic was synonymous with authentic, pre-industrial modes of labour and an honest relationship sustained between materials, craftsmen and, ultimately, God.

The third important theorist of the Gothic Revival was Viollet-le-Duc, whose work took a quite different direction to those of the more sentimentally-inclined revivals. In his *Entretiens sur l'architecture* (1863–72; translated as *Discourses on Architecture*, 1877–81), he argued that architecture must be based on structural principles and fidelity to the intrinsic properties of materials, be they traditional or modern. Although he maintained that form was of secondary consideration, it was in the Gothic that he saw these principles at work most clearly. Although Viollet-le-Duc's theories were not always borne out successfully in his architecture, his structural rationalism and truth to materials proved influential on Modernist thinking.

Restitutive Gothic

The Cambridge Camden Society, later renamed the Ecclesiological Society after it moved to London, was prominent in the 1830s and 1840s for its declarations that the spirit and religious order of the Middle Ages could be recaptured through a revival of Gothic architecture. Accuracy was, therefore, key, with numerous rules for architects to follow set out in its *A Few Words to Church-builders* (1841).

Structural Gothic

Viollet-le-Duc argued that a building's form should ultimately reflect its structure, while the materials used to construct it should be employed in such a way that remained true to their intrinsic qualities. He argued that if modern materials could create huge spans and tall structures, as seen for example in his design for a concert hall, then these constituted the uses to which they should rationally be put.

A.W.N. Pugin, St. Giles Catholic Church, Cheadle, Cheshire, 1841–6

Eugène-Emmanuel Viollet-le-Duc, design for a concert hall (ca. 1866) from *Entretiens sur l'architecture* (1863–72)

Natural Gothic

The skeletal systems of animals and plants
were often examined for inspiration for
'natural' Gothic structures, notably by
Viollet-le-Duc. The slender Gothicized
iron forms of the roof of Oxford's Natural
History Museum echo the skeletons
exhibited beneath, while references to
the science of geology were made through
the use of different stones throughout
the museum building.

Thomas Deane and Benjamin Woodward,
Natural History Museum, Oxford, 1854–8

Eclectic Gothic

While he was also known for a number of
church commissions, G.E. Street's magnum
opus is undoubtedly the Royal Courts of
Justice in London. His design constitutes
a kind of synthesis of both the styles and
the forms of English Gothic, reflective of the
spirit of the age that saw the establishment
of natural English law.

G.E. Street, Royal Courts of Justice, London,
1868–82

Ruskinian Gothic

Ruskin celebrated the Gothic's ornamental variety for the freedom it offered the craftsman's individual creativity. What he advocated therefore was an evolution of the Gothic rather than a straightforward revival of its medieval incarnation. The rich polychromy and structural use of brick in All Saints, Margaret Street, by William Butterfield (1814–1900), a favourite of the Ecclesiological Society, reflected Ruskin's ideas.

Modern Gothic

New building types and technologies presented opportunities for applying and adapting the Gothic in new ways. George Gilbert Scott's Midland Grand Hotel (now the St. Pancras Renaissance London Hotel), one of the world's most up-to-date hotels when it was completed, presents a Gothic face to St. Pancras Station and the soaring yet almost entirely astylar train shed behind, which was designed by William Henry Barlow (1812–1902).

William Butterfield, All Saints, Margaret Street, London, 1850–59

George Gilbert Scott, Midland Grand Hotel, London, 1865–76

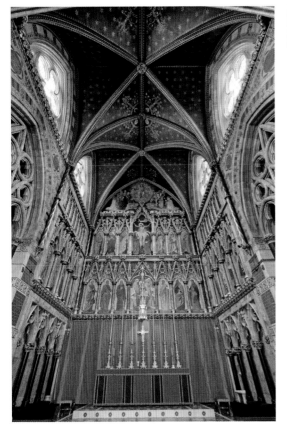

Region: Europe and the United States
Period: Mid-eighteenth to early twentieth century
Characteristics: Indian; Egyptian; Moorish; Mayan; Chinese; Imperialist

The interactions between East and West brought on by colonialist expansion have had a long and wide-ranging impact on architecture. Until the emergence of Modernism, and in some cases after, the relationship between East and West, architectural or otherwise, was governed by one overriding framework: Orientalism. In his landmark book *Orientalism* (1978), the post-colonial theorist Edward Said argued that from the first contact with colonial explorers, non-Western cultures had been perceived and were frequently represented as a singular, fictionalized 'Orient'. Centuries of imperialist expansion had seen such cultures submit through military force to being 'Orientalized' by the West. While Western cultures viewed themselves as paragons of civilization, learning and progress, the 'Orient' was associated with barbarity, the supposed ignorance of its people, and cultural and intellectual stasis. By defining Western culture by what it was not, it was through Orientalism, Said argued, that the idea of 'the West' came into existence as a coherent entity.

Cultural (including architectural) figurations of Orientalism began almost as soon as the first encounters between different cultures. The 'new worlds' were quickly exploited for their riches; international commercial organizations such as the British and Dutch East India Companies forged sophisticated trade routes, not just for commodities such as tea and spices, but for more valuable cultural goods such as porcelain. Alluringly Oriental Chinese blue-and-white ceramic wares, for example, became fashionable all over Europe for much of the seventeenth and eighteenth centuries.

Initially, architectural experiments with Oriental styles largely took place in the culturally and socially controlled environments of landscape gardens, where they formed part of broader Picturesque fantasies. The Royal Pavilion in Brighton, Sussex, designed by John Nash for George, Prince of Wales (who became Prince Regent and later George IV), was one of the first major statements of Orientalist architecture; its exotic Mughal-influenced exterior and sumptuous chinoiserie interiors were clearly symbolic of British imperial authority over India. Orientalist architecture became more diverse through the nineteenth and into the twentieth century, largely as consequence of broader stylistic eclecticism and the commercial opportunities presented in building in Egyptian, Moorish or even Mayan styles.

Imperialist architecture in the colonies themselves faced a quite different situation. In their laying out of New Delhi, which from 1911 was the administrative capital for the British Raj, Sir Edwin Lutyens (1869–1944) and Sir Herbert Baker (1862–1946) drew on the English Baroque for their monumental forms, infused with carefully deployed references to Indian architecture. Although in many ways a representation of British imperialism, their monumental vocabulary has proved flexible enough to have been co-opted to suit the needs of the independent Indian state.

Indian

The Mughal Style developed in the reign
of the Mughal Emperor Akbar the Great
(r. 1556–1605) was of great interest to
British architects not only because of its
soaring domes and decorative flourishes
but also because of its symmetry, which
related it to Western classical tradition.
John Nash's Royal Pavilion is heavily
influenced by the Mughal tradition, which it
fuses with elements of Islamic architecture.

John Nash, Royal Pavilion,
Brighton, 1787–1823

Egyptian

Napoleon's Egyptian campaigns created a burst of interest in all things Egyptian in Europe and also in the United States. The Washington Memorial, a soaring obelisk begun in 1848 and the tallest man-made structure in the world when finally competed in 1884, was the most conspicuous example of a number of Egyptian-inspired works intended to represent permanence and universality, perceived as synonymous with the young state.

Thomas Stewart, Egyptian Building, Medical College of Virginia, Richmond, Virginia, completed 1845

Moorish

The horseshoe arches, layered façades and abstract brick patterns of Islamic Moorish architecture, notably the great fourteenth-century palace of the Alhambra in Granada, Spain (see page 81), particularly fascinated European and American architects in the nineteenth and early twentieth centuries. Moorish domes and minarets, symbols of luxury and glamour, adorned a number of hotels and theatres in the United States.

John A. Wood, Tampa Bay Hotel (now Henry B. Plant Museum, University of Tampa), Tampa, Florida, 1888–91

Mayan

Pre-Columbian Mesoamerican architecture was of great interest to numerous American architects during the 1920s and 1930s. Mayan culture provided a decidedly indigenous reference for architects who sought to move beyond the European tradition. Several of Frank Lloyd Wright's California houses abstracted the essence of Mayan architecture, while Robert Stacy-Judd (1884–1975) fused its decorative language with Art Deco forms.

Robert Stacy-Judd, Aztec Hotel, Monrovia, California, 1924

Chinese

Unlike the vast majority of architects, Sir William Chambers had actually visited China (and also Bengal, India) when he worked for the Swedish East India Company. He was engaged as architectural tutor to the Prince of Wales, later George III (r. 1760–1820), whose sister Princess Augusta later employed him as an architect at Kew. Chambers designed a number of buildings for the gardens there, including a ten-storey pagoda to which he applied his knowledge of Chinese architecture.

Imperialist

Lutyens's Viceroy's House stands as the culmination of the ceremonial and administrative centre of the city of New Delhi that he laid out with Sir Herbert Baker. While strongly influenced by the work of Sir Christopher Wren, notably both built and unbuilt schemes for Greenwich Hospital in London, Lutyens also incorporated references to native Indian architecture: polychromy, decorative details and *chhatris* (open dome-like forms).

Sir William Chambers, Pagoda,
Royal Botanic Gardens, Kew,
London, 1761

Sir Edwin Lutyens, Rashtrapati Bhavan
(formerly the Viceroy's House), New Delhi,
India, 1912–30

Region: France and the United States
Period: Mid-nineteenth to early twentieth century
Characteristics: Imbricated façades; High façades; Iron structures; Axial planning; Civic buildings; Modern building types

The Beaux-Arts style takes its name from the École des Beaux-Arts in Paris, where many of the main exponents of the style studied. Others were exposed to its precepts at other architecture schools, especially those in the United States, that followed its methods and philosophy. The history of the École goes back to the seventeenth century. In 1648 Louis XIV's minister Cardinal Mazarin founded the Académie Royale de Peinture et de Sculpture. Its architectural counterpart, the Académie Royale d'Architecture, was founded in 1671 at the instigation of Mazarin's successor, Jean-Baptiste Colbert, who saw the potential of culture and especially architecture to embody and glorify the majesty of the Sun King. In 1816 the two institutions were merged to form the Académie des Beaux-Arts; the school was granted independence from government control in 1863 by Napoleon III, and was renamed the École des Beaux-Arts.

The philosophy of the school reflected this long history. The classical tradition both in art and architecture was the almost sole focus of its teaching. Unconcerned with matters of engineering and building construction, students studied ancient Greek and Roman architecture as well as some Renaissance and Baroque examples. Ateliers were run by practising architects, under whose guidance the students would learn a number of formal techniques. They would then work up initial sketches into often quite elaborate presentation drawings, which would then be offered to a panel or jury for a critique.

This rigidly academic teaching method resulted in a relatively consistent Beaux-Arts style. Grandly classical façades were layered with rich ornamentation and sculpture. Interior design largely reflected the architectural language of the exterior, adding elaborate gilding and the polychromatic effects of different types of polished marbles. Axial planning separated the grand, often ceremonial spaces from service areas. All of this contributed to a style of architecture that was theatre-like in its artificiality, yet rarely theatrical; its academically determined composition of ornament and sculpture verged on a concept of architecture as image.

The Beaux-Arts style was widely applied during the second half of the nineteenth century and well into the twentieth, especially in the United States. A number of influential architects, notably Henry Hobson Richardson (1838–86), Charles Follen McKim (1847–1909; of McKim, Mead & White) and the partners John Merven Carrère (1858–1911) and Thomas Hastings (1860–1929), had trained at the École in Paris, while several American schools adopted its teaching philosophies, the Massachusetts Institute of Technology being the first in 1892. A year later the Beaux-Arts influence in America was literally cemented by the famous 'White City' of the World's Columbian Exposition in Chicago, which marked the 400th anniversary of Christopher Columbus's voyage. Its grand boulevards, laid out by Daniel Burnham (1846–1912), and white Beaux-Arts buildings, lit at night by electric light, were intended to represent a particularly American kind of formality and a cultural counterpoint to the onslaught of modernity.

Imbricated façades

Beaux-Arts façades were usually imbricated, or layered with overlapping classical elements or sculpture, to provide coherence to the whole ensemble. The repeating sculptural adornments of Girault's Petit Palais link the otherwise separate components of its façade. The use of imbrication was a result of the way in which architectural ideas were worked up and presented in perspective presentation drawings in the Beaux-Arts tradition, with watercolour simulating the effects of light and shade.

Charles Girault, Petit Palais, Paris, 1896–1900

High façades

Beaux-Arts façades typically consisted of a high rusticated basement level, which acted as the building's lower storey; a tall piano nobile, usually articulated with an applied order with recessed arched openings; and a thick cornice and wide attic level, often adorned with reliefs. In particularly grand examples, such as the Palais Garnier, the whole ensemble would be topped by statues and sometimes a low dome.

Charles Garnier, Palais Garnier, Paris, 1861–74

Iron structures

Although he had trained at the École and was clearly part of the Beaux-Arts tradition, Henri Labrouste (1801–75) was also influenced by rationalist thinking about structure. A number of his works, including the reading rooms he designed for the Bibliothèque Sainte-Geneviève and slightly later at the Bibliothèque Nationale, make dramatic use of iron frameworks to create soaring interior spaces.

Henri Labrouste, Reading Room, Bibliothèque Nationale de France, Paris, 1862–8

Axial planning

Although Baron Haussmann (1809–91) was a planner rather than an architect, his rebuilding of Paris between 1883 and 1870 both drew from and informed the Beaux-Arts tradition. Haussmann demolished medieval fabric to make way for grand boulevards (wide enough, it was said, to prevent barricades). New monuments were positioned at the intersections, while the surroundings of existing monuments such as the Arc de Triomphe were made grander.

Baron Georges-Eugène Haussmann, Place de l'Étoile (now Place Charles de Gaulle), Paris, 1853–70

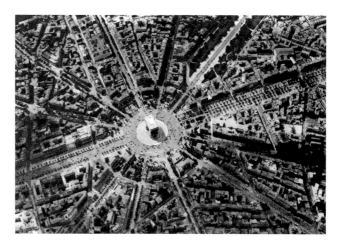

Civic buildings

Beaux-Arts architects were often commissioned to create great grand civic buildings symbolic of the self-confidence of a town or city. The monumental New York Public Library by Carrère and Hastings, one of the most distinguished American Beaux-Arts practices, was fairly typical of its mature work, which also included numerous private houses, many examples of commercial architecture and several urban plans.

Carrère and Hastings, New York Public Library, New York City, 1897–1911

Modern building types

The advent of modernity overturned the convention that a building's importance could be inferred through its scale. Factories, warehouses and railway stations all required vast structures, the construction of which often created significant disruption. Beaux-Arts architecture was often deployed in these situations to put a civil face on these new buildings.

Reed and Stem and Warren and Wetmore, Grand Central Terminal, New York City, 1903–13

Region: England, and also the United States
Period: Mid-nineteenth to early twentieth century
Characteristics: Vernacular; Picturesque sensibility; Domestic; Indigenous materials and crafts;
Decentralization; Garden Suburbs

The Arts and Crafts movement, led both spiritually and intellectually by William Morris, was an aesthetic and idealistic reaction to the forces and conditions of modernity. Influenced by Ruskin, Morris was committed to the reintegration of high aesthetics and everyday craftsmanship. A committed socialist with strong views on the dehumanizing effects of the division of labour, Morris argued that if the artist and architect became craftsmen once more, the tyranny of the machine could be overthrown. Despite his opposition to modernity (also reflected in his instrumental role in founding the Society for the Protection of Ancient Buildings in 1877), he found commercial, as well as artistic, success with his firm Morris & Co. making furniture, fabrics, carpets and wallpapers inspired by late medieval precedents. Morris revived numerous traditional skills, although he took care not to slavishly imitate the past but rather to revive its methods and remain true to its principles in an era of great change.

Architecturally the Arts and Crafts movement was characterized by a romantic historicism that harked back to a traditional rural lifestyle before the advent of modernity and the squalor of industrial cities. Traditional building crafts were combined with an eclectic range of architectural styles; Morris's own Red House, Kent, designed by Philip Webb (1831–1915) in 1859, for example, combined medieval influences with Queen Anne Style round-headed windows. The movement's other leading architects, particularly Richard Norman Shaw (1831–1912), were less opposed than Morris to modern forms, and combined sophisticated contemporary plans with styles ranging from half-timbering and Jacobean to Dutch Renaissance and English Baroque.

Arts and Crafts ideas had an international reach; in Germany Hermann Muthesius (1861–1927) was their leading advocate, with an important influence on the Deutscher Werkbund group of artists, architects, designers and industrialists. Of American architects, Henry Hobson Richardson was the most prominent of those whose work was directly informed by Arts and Crafts ideas, although they were also influential on his followers Louis Sullivan (1856–1924) and Frank Lloyd Wright (1869–1959).

In the nineteenth century there were numerous reactions to the impacts of modernity and alternative social and urban models proposed: from Charles Fourier's utopian visions to Saltaire, built near Leeds, Yorkshire, from 1851 by the industrialist Sir Titus Salt to provide respectable housing for his workers. Ebenezer Howard's *Tomorrow: A Peaceful Path to Real Reform* (1898), which inaugurated the influential Garden City movement, combined utopian optimism with a moral conviction borne from the overcrowding of industrial cities. Advocating a suburban model, with both abundant green space and homes close to centres of employment, Howard placed important emphasis on the family house, through which, he believed, a balance could be achieved between individual identity and the social relationships of an ideal town. Although Howard specified no particular architectural style, Letchworth Garden City, Hertfordshire, the first of these new towns, was largely populated by Arts and Crafts-style housing, reflecting the synergies between the two movements.

Vernacular

If any building could be said to constitute a 'manifesto' of the Arts and Crafts movement it is surely Morris's Red House in Bexleyheath. Constructed in red brick, and mixing medieval and Queen Anne styles, it eschewed the perceived façadism of high architecture in favour of a distinct focus on the vernacular, in which every component of the house (and garden) received the craftsmen's attention.

Philip Webb, Red House, Bexleyheath, Kent, England, 1859

Picturesque sensibility

Begun in 1875, Bedford Park in west London has a strong claim to be the first Garden Suburb. Its pioneering owner, Jonathan Carr, commissioned the leading architect Richard Norman Shaw to produce a number of house designs for the new development. Shaw's designs, largely in the Queen Anne Style, created streets that, although entirely new, possessed a natural, Picturesque variety – a recurring feature of Arts and Crafts design.

Richard Norman Shaw, Bedford Park Garden Suburb, London, 1875–86

Domestic

For Arts and Crafts architects, it was through the individual house that craftsmanship and design could be linked directly to the patterns of everyday life, an idea that had important implications for Modernism. M.H. Baillie Scott's Blackwell, designed as a holiday retreat for the Manchester brewer Sir Edward Holt, achieves a harmonious domesticity through a balanced design and use of materials, and incorporates furniture by Morris & Co. and Charles Voysey (1857–1941).

M.H. Baillie Scott, Blackwell, Bowness-on-Windermere, Cumbria, England, 1898–1900

Indigenous materials and crafts

The comparative simplicity of Voysey's designs belied the highly refined sensibility of their craftsmanship. At Broad Leys he made use of local stone, creating large bow windows to provide views of the Cumbrian landscape. His use of wide-banded windows and plain surfaces was seen by the architectural historian Nikolaus Pevsner as prefiguring equivalent forms in Modernism, although Voysey himself rejected this interpretation of his work.

Charles Voysey, Broad Leys, Windermere, Cumbria, 1898

Decentralization

Garden Cities were intended to offer an alternative to the density and centralization of modern industrial cities. They made early use of zoning systems to separate industrial, residential and green areas in such a way that enhanced the quality of life of residents while recognizing the necessity of local centres of employment. The result, as demonstrated at Letchworth Garden City, was a town almost entirely suburban in character.

Raymond Unwin and Barry Parker, Letchworth Garden City, Hertfordshire, begun 1903

Garden Suburbs

While borrowing heavily from Howard's ideas, the concept of the Garden Suburb was in fact a reversion of his philosophy; as additions to cities, such suburbs indirectly exacerbated the conditions that Howard sought to alleviate. While part of London, Hampstead Garden Suburb aimed to create a suburban idyll populated with Arts and Crafts houses; later, some Modernist homes were also built there, representing the influence of Garden City ideas on Modernist planning.

G.G. Winbourne, Lytton Close, Hampstead Garden Suburb, Barnet (now London), 1934–6

Region: Europe, especially Brussels, Paris and Vienna
Period: Late nineteenth to early twentieth century
Characteristics: Organic forms; Articulating modernity; Symbolism; Material contrasts; Anti-historicism; Anti-ornament

Emerging at the end of the nineteenth century and prevalent until the outbreak of World War I in 1914, Art Nouveau was arguably the first avant-garde architectural style. Rejecting historicism, if not tradition itself, Art Nouveau, or Jugendstil as it was known in Germany, encompassed all areas of design and the decorative arts. The sensation of the 1900 Paris Exposition Universelle, the style quickly became an international phenomenon, perhaps due in part to its dissemination in print and graphic design. It had, however, first emerged in Belgium in the work of Victor Horta (1861–1947) and Henry van de Velde (1863–1957), best exemplified in the former's three hotels in Brussels built during the 1890s and the pioneering, though now destroyed, Maison du Peuple, the headquarters for the Belgian socialist party.

In many ways Art Nouveau provided a connection between the inherent subjectivity of craft and the objectivity of modern mechanized production. The former position was exemplified by the designs of the Catalan architect Antoni Gaudí (1852–1926), whose work was only loosely affiliated with Art Nouveau. Inspired by Ruskin, Gaudí looked towards the Gothic, in particular, to create a specifically Catalan architecture based on complex symbolism and geometry, and rendered through individual craftsmanship. Hector Guimard's Paris Métro station entrances, in contrast, presented the adherence to the objective position, deploying Art Nouveau forms to communicate the presence of new modern infrastructure.

By the 1900s many architects previously aligned with Art Nouveau were moving beyond its formal language. One of the most significant works exhibiting this tendency was Charles Rennie Mackintosh's Glasgow School of Art (1897–1909). Making unconventional use of the site's steep slope, Mackintosh created a succession of different spaces, each lit according their function (north light for studios, top-lighting for the museum spaces). His interior palette of wood and iron created dynamic material juxtapositions in a building that, while reminiscent of Art Nouveau in style, was startlingly original in its handling of space and light.

Although Mackintosh's work received little initial attention in Britain, it was influential on the Vienna Secession, the group of artists and architects formed in 1897 who had resigned in protest from the conservative Vienna Künstlerhaus. Otto Wagner's *Moderne Architektur* (1895) was a important text for the Secession; it argued in favour of an architecture that, in keeping with the philosophy of Art Nouveau, rejected historicism, but that should also represent modernity using appropriate materials and techniques. Secessionist buildings, such as Wagner's Post Office Savings Bank (1894–1902), tended to be plain, eschewing much of the ornament associated with Art Nouveau. This attempt to forge a modern culture, free from the contingencies of ornament, was taken to its logical conclusion by Adolf Loos in his famous essay, 'Ornament and Crime' (1908).

Organic forms

Art Nouveau design is most readily
identified by its preponderance of flowing
organic forms, such as flowers, vines and
leaves, most often represented in ironwork
– in many ways a conscious reaction to
Beaux-Arts academicism. The stairway of
Horta's Hôtel Tassel in Brussels deploys
these forms structurally to create a sense
of tension and movement.

Victor Horta, Hôtel Tassel, Brussels, 1892–3

Articulating modernity

Unmistakably associated with the *Belle
Époque*, Guimard's designs for the Paris
Métro stations were essentially mass
produced; their novel sinewy organic forms
were the manifestation above ground of
the modernity of the new transport system.
Guimard's structures were influenced by
Viollet-le-Duc, largely following the latter's
structural rationalist theories but without
any predisposition towards the Gothic.

Hector Guimard, Porte Dauphine Métro
Station, Paris, 1900

Symbolism

Each level of Gaudí's masterwork, the Sagrada Familia in Barcelona, increases in fantasy, moving towards and then beyond Art Nouveau. Drawing from North African Berber architecture as well as Gothic and organic forms, Gaudí created a dynamic tension between the rationalism of Barcelona's grid and his almost metaphysical architecture that alludes to the work of the Surrealists, notably his fellow Catalan Salvador Dalí.

Material contrasts

In his library at the Glasgow School of Art, built slightly later than the rest of the school, Mackintosh inserted a mezzanine level around the perimeter of the double-height space, supported by brackets. Along with the bookcases and furniture, the bracket forms create dynamic lines and contrasts between material and light – an abstract manifestation of a recurring Art Nouveau characteristic.

Antoni Gaudí, Expiatory Church of the Holy Family (Sagrada Familia), Barcelona, Spain, begun 1884

Charles Rennie Mackintosh, Library, Glasgow School of Art, Glasgow, Scotland, 1908

Anti-historicism

The artists and architects of the Vienna
Secession reacted specifically against the
conservative historicism of the Vienna
Künstlerhaus and more broadly against
the staid mid-nineteenth-century buildings
along the prominent Ringstrasse. Joseph
Maria Olbrich's stark Secession Building,
with interior decorations by the painter
Gustav Klimt, was the architectural
manifestation of the new spirit promoted
by the Secession and summarized in
the title of its publication, *Ver Sacrum*
(Sacred Spring, 1898–1903).

Joseph Maria Olbrich, Secession Building,
Vienna, 1897–8

Anti-ornament

While for Adolf Loos wasting time and
effort on ornament was tantamount to
a crime, there was a recognition that
decoration – for example, sculpture or
painting – could help a building convey
meaning. Josef Hoffman's Palais
Stoclet in Brussels, designed for the
industrialist and art collector Adolphe
Stoclet, largely rejected ornament, but
through decoration and architectural form
it was able to sustain many different ideas
and interpretations.

Josef Hoffman, Palais Stoclet, Brussels,
1905–11

Region: United States, and also Europe
Period: 1920s and 1930s
Characteristics: Speed and movement; Glamour; Rectilinear; Exoticism; Residual classicism; Geometric forms

Art Deco burst onto the world stage at the Exposition Internationale des Arts Décoratifs et Industriels Modernes in Paris in 1925. The underlying aim of the exhibition, which gave Art Deco its name, was to re-establish Paris as the leading centre of design, fashion and high-end consumer products. National pavilions, as well as ones for leading designers and department stores, showcased fashionable wares in the exhibition itself, while the whole of Paris was brought into its orbit with elaborate displays ornamenting the shop windows of the city's boulevards, and its streets, bridges and park dramatically lit at night. Even the Eiffel Tower was adorned with the logo of the Citroën car company – an overt symbol of consumerism as well as of French industry and design.

The exhibition organizers had asked for submissions that were 'modern'. Despite this the displays at many pavilions, including the Swedish, Dutch and French, sat astride the two poles of tradition and modernity, an inherent contradiction that in many ways defined Art Deco. Pierre Patout's acclaimed display pavilion, called the Hôtel d'un Collectionneur, with its interior suite of rooms designed by Jacques-Emile Ruhlmann, exemplified this paradox. For its Grand Salon Ruhlmann brought together some of the leading Parisian artists and designers to create a room boldly modern in its design yet harking back to historical tradition through its oval form and its very status as a salon.

The exhibition was also notable for its Modernist displays. Le Corbusier (1887–1966) exhibited his infamous Plan Voisin inside his Pavillon de l'Esprit Nouveau, while the Constructivist Soviet pavilion by Konstantin Melnikov (1890–1974) showcased the bold artistic experiments taking place in post-Revolutionary Russia. In contrast to these pioneering Modernist experiments, Art Deco, as it both appeared in the exhibition and developed over the next decade, was almost entirely devoid of intellectual content or of a social or a moral agenda. It was style in its purest sense, and reactionary in its undiscerning embrace of eclectic ornament, colour, rich materials and lustrous surfaces.

If anything, Art Deco represented a vague optimism in the possibilities of modernity, not as a break from the past (as did Modernism), but in a way that democratized – or rather – 'consumerized' luxury. Architecture – notably in new theatres and cinemas – was just one manifestation of Art Deco, which was also used for the design of everything from ocean liners and cars through to telephones and radios. Art Deco epitomized the excitement and glamour of the Jazz Age and the fashionable, party-going 'Bright Young Things', satirized by the English writer Evelyn Waugh in his novel *Vile Bodies* (1930).

Speed and movement

Art Deco embodied the speed of the
modern age, drawing from as well as
informing the design of cars, trains and
ocean liners. The architectural equivalent
was undoubtedly the skyscraper, and in
particular William Van Alen's majestic
Chrysler Building. Constructed in a short
space of time, it became, for a few months,
the world's tallest building.

William Van Alen, Chrysler Building,
New York City, 1928–30

Glamour

London's first truly curtain-walled building, the restrained exterior – of smooth Vitrolite and glass set between chromium strips – of Sir Owen Williams's Daily Express Building belies its glamorous entrance, in which Robert Atkinson deployed the full repertoire of Art Deco effects. Gilding, silver, a huge shining pendant and exotic reliefs by Eric Aumonier combined to dazzle the advertising men delivering their copy and illustrations.

Ellis & Clarke with Sir Owen Williams
(entrance hall by Robert Atkinson),
Daily Express Building, London, 1929–33

Rectilinear

While Art Nouveau was characterized by curving, sinewy, organic forms, Art Deco architecture was on the whole rectilinear. In part, this was due to the residual influence of Beaux-Arts axial planning, but it was also a result of the rectilinear frames used to realize the types of interior spaces required for modern building types such as factories.

Wallis Gilbert and Partners, Hoover Factory,
Perivale, London, 1935

Exoticism

The Daily Telegraph Building in Napier, built after an earthquake in 1931 destroyed much of the city, followed Art Deco fashion in its allusions to Egyptian architecture through applied pilasters and decoration. Such references – and those to Mayan and Asian architecture, among others – frequently appeared in Art Deco, a sign of the allure and increasing accessibility of international travel.

Ernest Arthur Williams, Daily Telegraph
Building, Napier, New Zealand, 1932

Residual classicism

While Art Deco evoked modernity, it was often underlaid by a classical sense of order, detectable in its planning. The work of the English architect Charles Holden (1876–1960), which was only loosely Art Deco, elegantly combined a classical sensibility with modern forms and planning; the most notable examples are his stations for the London Underground, including Arnos Grove, which was inspired by Gunnar Asplund's Stockholm Public Library in Sweden.

Charles Holden, Arnos Grove Underground Station, London, 1932

Geometric forms

Like its rectilinearity, Art Deco's geometric forms were in stark contrast to the flowing curves of Art Nouveau. Zigzags, chevrons, concentric arches and other forms appear frequently, often inlaid with modern materials such as Bakelite (a type of plastic) or aluminium. The concentric arches of the Radio City Music Hall – the best-known of a huge number of Art Deco theatres and cinemas – focus attention dynamically towards the stage.

Edward Durell Stone (interior design by Donald Deskey), Radio City Music Hall, Rockefeller Center, New York City, 1932

Modernism

Throughout the nineteenth century architects had debated how, and indeed whether, the advances in technology created by the Industrial Revolution should be reflected in architecture. What is now broadly understood as Modernism emerged from the conclusion that architecture should not only reflect the spirit of the modern age but also that it had a moral obligation to do so. As the cultural response to the conditions of modernity, Modernism, it was argued, had the power to transform how people lived, worked and, fundamentally, understood and responded to the world around them.

Vers une architecture

Despite early experiments it was really not until after World War I that architecture fully embraced Modernism. In 1918 the Swiss-born architect Charles-Édouard Jeanneret (1887–1966), soon to adopt the pseudonym by which he is better known, Le Corbusier, published the manifesto *Après le cubisme*, with the painter Amédée Ozenfant. Together they rejected Cubism's insistence on fragmentation and instead argued that the concept of volume should be privileged above all other qualities of objects.

A few years later, in 1923, appeared Le Corbusier's most seminal text, *Vers une architecture*, the impact of which is arguably still being felt. He called on architects to reject the traditional and to embrace new values fit for the modern age, ones that he saw already deployed by the designers of ocean liners, aeroplanes and the *sine qua non* of modernity, the car. He articulated 'Five Points' – essentially organizing principles – which would govern the new architecture: buildings should be raised on thin piers, or *piloti;* structural support could then be separated from the division of space both within and without, allowing the façade to be 'free' and the plan 'open' (the second and third principles); long ribbon windows would provide abundant daylight; and a roof garden would restore the ground area occupied by the building. Best illustrated in Le Corbusier's domestic architecture, the 'Five Points' proved highly influential across numerous building types.

Although Le Corbusier claimed that much of what he advocated was radically new, other important architects in Germany such as Walter Gropius (1883–1969) and Ludwig Mies van der Rohe (1886–1969), who had trained with Le Corbusier under Peter Behrens (1868–1940), were also making strides in advancing the Modernist cause, and became the leading figures of the so-called Modern Movement. Gropius founded the pioneering Bauhaus school in Weimar in 1919, which in its fluid combination of art, craft and industrial design had important parallels with contemporary artistic institutions in the Soviet Union. The relocation of the Bauhaus to Dessau in 1925 gave Gropius the opportunity to design its new building, which immediately became an icon of Modernist architecture. Mies himself was director from 1930 until the school was closed by the Nazi regime in 1933.

International Modernism

In 1932 an exhibition held at the Museum of Modern Art (MoMA) in New York (and which later toured the United States) organized by the historian Henry-Russell Hitchcock and the architect Philip Johnson (1906–2005) thrust Modernism onto the global stage. The exhibition grouped the architecture of Le Corbusier, Mies and Gropius alongside that of the American Frank Lloyd Wright (1869–1959) as the new 'International Style'. It was, however, following World War II that Modernist architecture became truly international, developing in ever more different directions as architects grappled with the essential question of how to generate the appropriate form for buildings in the modern age. Modernism's broad social agenda drove much of the rebuilding programme in Europe after the war; the destruction ironically gave architects the opportunity to realize their ambition of rebuilding the world anew.

Chicago School

Expressionism

New Objectivity

International Style

Functionalism

Constructivism

**Totalitarian
Reactions**

Essentialism

Brutalism

Metabolism

High-Tech

Region: United States
Period: 1880s to 1900s
Characteristics: Steel frame; Rectilinear façades; Cuboidal form; Height; Classically derived decoration; Stone facing

While the skyscraper became synonymous with New York over the course of the twentieth century, it was in Chicago that this archetypically modern building type was born in the final decades of the nineteenth. Chicago's early importance lay in its role as the gateway to the western United States, which had been increasingly opened up by railways from the mid nineteenth century. In 1871 a great fire laid waste to much of the city's centre. The destruction and subsequent rebuilding inadvertently provided the opportunity to cement Chicago's position as one of America's most important cities, economically and architecturally.

The Chicago School – a group of leading architects working in the city around the turn of the century – is not usually thought of as Modernist, at least in the conventional sense. However, if one considers the essential problem posed by Modernism as one of how to generate the appropriate form for buildings that would reflect both their modern construction and the spirit of the new age, then the Chicago School architects were among the first to grapple with it.

In an essay published in 1896 entitled 'The Tall Office Building Artistically Considered', Louis Sullivan (1856–1924), the most famous architect of the Chicago School, argued that tall buildings should actively embrace this characteristic; their dominant architectural expression should be one of verticality. The essay articulated something of a post-rationalization for what Sullivan and others had already been doing in Chicago for more than ten years. The cuboidal form of the First Leiter Building (1879) by William Le Baron Jenney (1832–1907) was treated as single coherent entity, with its steel frame and regular floor structure expressed on its exterior. Marshall Field's Wholesale Store (1885–7) by Henry Hobson Richardson matched the grid structure of Jenney's earlier building with a monumental abstract classicism. Vaguely reminiscent of a Renaissance *palazzo*, the Marshall Field building announced its modernity through the sheer scale of its steel-frame structure behind a rough-hewn stone façade.

What is arguably the most enduring work of the Chicago School – Dankmar Adler (1844–1900) and Louis Sullivan's Wainwright Building (1890–91) – was actually built in St. Louis, Missouri. Despite a number of structural conceits, its underlying steel frame is reflected externally in a repeating grid to which all other elements, including a loosely classical detailing, are subservient. The Wainwright Building's unerring insistence on verticality, as an expression of the new possibilities of its modern construction, was to become a recurring theme of Modernist architecture.

Steel frame

Consisting in their simplest form of series of regularly spaced vertical posts joined by horizontal beams, steel-frame structures allowed more freedom in the configuration of interior spaces as walls were no longer the main load-bearing elements. The Reliance Building's steel frame facilitated the early use of a glass curtain wall, inaugurating a formal lineage to the Mies-inspired post-war work of the Chicago practice of Skidmore, Owings & Merrill (SOM).

Rectilinear façades

When reflected in the building's exterior, the trabeated steel frame produced rectilinear buildings and façades characterized by a grid structure of horizontal floor lines and vertical supports, with windows set between them. Sullivan compartmentalized the grid structure so that retail space occupied the building's base level and offices were stacked above, with a central core for circulation and a lift (elevator) turn-around at the top.

Burnham & Root (main designer
Charles Atwood), Reliance Building,
Chicago, 1890–94

Adler & Sullivan,
Guaranty Building, Buffalo,
New York, 1894–5

Cuboidal form

Steel frames allowed buildings to be constructed quickly and often more cheaply, with many standardized components. When multiplied the trabeated system of vertical posts and horizontal beams resulted in a cuboidal form, with evenly spaced floors and flat roofs. The cuboidal form became one of the defining morphologies of Modernist architecture.

William Le Baron Jenney, Leiter II Building, Chicago, completed 1889

Height

Early 'skyscrapers' were in fact not particularly tall: they were dwarfed by the 308-metre-high (1,010-feet-high) Eiffel Tower, Paris (1889), and were lower even than some church spires. However, what they offered from a relatively small ground plan was large amounts of habitable space, newly accessible thanks to the advent of lifts (elevators) – economically advantageous where land prices were high, such as in the Chicago Loop, the site of many early skyscrapers.

William Le Baron Jenney, Home Insurance Building, Chicago, completed 1884

Classically derived decoration

With little in the way of an indigenous architectural tradition (although Latin America was sometimes an inspiration), American architects had to draw from European examples for their decorative schemes, but they also enjoyed a freedom that came from being detached from the European tradition. Many Chicago School buildings had both modern features and an abstracted, often raw classicism.

Adler & Sullivan, Auditorium Building, Chicago, 1886–9

Stone facing

Despite their steel frames, stone, brick and moulded terracotta were commonly used on the façades of Chicago School buildings, and were combined with increasing and unprecedented areas of glass. The rough-hewn stone of Richardson's Marshall Field building recalled the rocky outcrops of the American landscape, sitting between the vernacular tradition and modernity.

Henry Hobson Richardson, Marshall Field's Wholesale Store, Chicago, 1885–7

Region: Germany and the Netherlands
Period: 1910s to mid 1920s
Characteristics: Expressive forms; Modern building types; Naturalism; Dynamism; Functionalism; Monolithic materials

The political, economic and social upheavals that followed Germany's defeat in World War I resulted in an overturning of old certainties, notably those embodied in the imperial order but also generally in assumptions about the direction of technological progress. Modernist architecture had begun to gain a foothold in Germany before the war, but the defeat and its aftermath irrevocably changed its course.

The economic turmoil and scarcity of resources in the immediate aftermath of the war confined most architects to paper in their attempts to visualize a rebuilt society. Bruno Taut's *Alpine Architektur* (1919) conjured a bold utopian vision of apparently glass buildings rising like mountain peaks in an explosion of light, symbolic of a return to a perceived natural order. In the same year as Taut's work was published Walter Gropius founded the Bauhaus, which in many ways sought to answer his call of 1913 that 'the new times demand their own expression'. Yet much of the early output of the Bauhaus, especially that produced by students under the direction of the Swiss painter Johannes Itten, was marked by a 'primitivist' streak. This reflected the ideas concerning the connection between form and certain mental states of another Bauhaus teacher, the Russian painter and theorist Wassily Kandinsky, published in 1912 in *Concerning the Spiritual in Art*. Like the interest of the anti-art Dada movement in cult, in many ways this approach constituted a Modernist retrenchment in response to the horrors of mechanized warfare.

Expressionist architecture emerged from this context and became identified in the early 1920s with a number of architects working in the Netherlands – the best-known being Michel de Klerk (1884–1923) and Pieter Kramer – and in Germany, notably Hans Poelzig (1869–1936), Fritz Höger (1877–1949) and Peter Behrens. Early work by Gropius and even Mies van der Rohe could be considered Expressionist, but for them, as for many architects in this period, Expressionism quickly gave way to Functionalist and rationalist approaches.

The architect most closely – and enduringly – associated with Expressionism is Erich Mendelsohn (1887–1953), his Einstein Tower in Potsdam, Germany (1920–24), being undoubtedly the movement's greatest work. Built to contain an observatory and astrophysics laboratory, the Tower stands almost as a work of sculpture, a single monolithic entity in a plastic, free-flowing form. Yet, the Tower's organic form is also determined by functional requirements; it acts as a telescope, with the cupola reflecting cosmic rays to the underground laboratory. This synthesis of the imaginative and the practical – essentially of formalism and Functionalism – largely defined Expressionist architecture. Even as Mendelsohn, like others, tempered his later designs with more conventional Modernist forms – seen, for example, in his De La Warr Pavilion, Bexhill, Sussex (1935; designed with Serge Chermayeff), his work always retained an individually sculptural quality.

Expressive forms

The defining characteristic of Expressionist architecture was its use of free-flowing, organic forms. Curves, odd angles, irregularly shaped windows and doors, and multi-layered façades were combined by the architects' imaginative intuition to create buildings that affected the emotions as much as the intellect.

Modern building types

From structures for industrial and scientific uses, to department stores and housing developments, Expressionist architects were frequently commissioned to design specifically modern types of building. Peter Behrens's industrial buildings, including the Hoechst Dye Works with its idiosyncratic clock tower, and for the German electrical equipment manufacturer AEG, sought to establish a kind of architectural corporate identity, an idea that became hugely influential after World War II.

Fritz Höger, Chilehaus, Hamburg, Germany, 1922–4

Peter Behrens, Hoechst Dye Works, Frankfurt am Main, Germany, 1920–25

Naturalism

A recurring feature of Expressionist architecture was its relationship to natural, especially geological, forms. Bruno Taut's *Alpine Architektur* (1919) had shown designs for architecture in a utopian mountainscape, with crystal-like buildings rising among the peaks. The Goetheanum and several other buildings by the Austrian philosopher, social reformer and architect Rudolf Steiner (1861–1925) partially realized Taut's vision.

Rudolf Steiner, Goetheanum, Dornach, Switzerland, 1924–8

Dynamism

The term 'dynamism' defined Mendelsohn's belief in fusing organic form with modern materials. Although his buildings appeared to have little in common with more rationalist, overtly rectilinear forms of Modernism, he frequently employed Modernist materials and features. Part of the drama of his works comes from his exploitation and subversion of the properties of steel and concrete in tension and compression.

Erich Mendelsohn, Einstein Tower, Potsdam, Germany, 1920–24

Functionalism

Expressionism's free-flowing forms were not simply the product of an architect's imagination but in most cases were also partly determined by functional requirements. Mendelsohn enlivened the potentially dull industrial building he was commissioned to design at Luckenwalde by architecturally animating the belt and pulley mechanisms through architectural design in a way that was quite distinct from that of harsher, later Functionalist buildings.

Erich Mendelsohn, Hat Factory and Dye Works, Luckenwalde, Germany, 1921–3

Monolithic materials

Often Expressionist buildings made
aesthetic use of just one material.
Mendelsohn's Einstein Tower was unified
as one monolithic entity by its smooth
veneer of white render, which gave it an
overtly sculptural quality. Brick, tile and
ceramic were also used, especially by Dutch
architects, for example by Michel de Klerk
in his masterwork, the Eigen Haard housing
development in Amsterdam.

Michel de Klerk, Het Schip,
Eigen Haard housing,
Amsterdam, completed 1921

Region: Germany
Period: Mid 1920s to mid 1930s
Characteristics: Rectilinearity; Rationality; Steel, concrete and glass; Planar surfaces; Industrial mass production; Continuous blocks

The influential Modernist magazine *G: Materials for Elemental Form-Creation* was first published in 1923. Largely driven by their rejection of the formalism associated with Expressionism, the magazine's founders, who included Mies van der Rohe, argued that form should be determined by objective rationalism, economy, and modern technology and methods of construction. This outlook became known as Neue Sachlichkeit – commonly translated as New Objectivity – and characterized trends in visual art and photography as well as in architecture.

At the Bauhaus Gropius had similarly begun to move the school's teaching away from its earlier Expressionist leanings to address the fundamental problem of how to unite industry and the arts to create an aesthetic reflecting the spirit of the age. Johannes Itten was replaced by the Hungarian photographer and designer Laszlo Moholy-Nagy (1895–1946) whose innovations stretched across a range of media. Under the influence of Moholy-Nagy and probably also as a result of the visit of the leading De Stijl artist Theo van Doesburg in 1922, the school's formal language was increasingly concerned with abstract, geometric arrangements of rectilinear forms. This approach was similar in some ways to the formal experiments then taking place at VKhUTEMAS in the Soviet Union (see page 170).

With the move to objectivity appar–ently complete, Gropius proclaimed, on the occasion of the Bauhaus exhibition of 1923: 'The Bauhaus believes the machine to be our modern medium of design and seeks to come to terms with it.' The opportunity of putting these bold aspirations into built form came when the Bauhaus moved from Weimar to Dessau in 1925. Gropius's design for the new building conceived it as a series of intersecting cuboid volumes with radical steel and glass façades, while internal spaces were configured according to their function and lighting requirements – a powerful articulation of his belief in architecture as the sphere in which the arts and the objectivity of industry could be readily fused.

By the mid 1920s Germany's economy was recovering and thoughts turned towards large-scale, low-cost housing developments. Arguably the most influential was Stuttgart's famous Weissenhofsiedlung. In 1925 Mies van der Rohe was asked to oversee an exhibition for the Deutscher Werkbund (German Work Federation) dedicated to new housing prototypes. Mies's scheme was loosely informed by Garden City principles (see page 136) of providing decent, humane living spaces for the mass of the population, and more specifically influenced by the innovative housing developments in Rotterdam and the Hook of Holland by J.J.P. Oud (1890–1963). Mies involved in the exhibition a number of eminent German architects, including Gropius, Taut (who had retreated from his earlier Expressionist phase), Hans Scharoun (1893–1972) and Hans Poelzig, and also some other Europeans, including Oud and Le Corbusier. Although each architect's project was conceived individually, all the designs were united by their white surfaces, *piloti* and wide-span windows. The architecture of each building was clearly and objectively expressed through its form and volume, inaugurating a type that proved influential for decades to come.

Rectilinearity

In contrast to the often curving forms of
Expressionism, rectilinearity – that is, the
arrangement of straight lines and planes
– defined Neue Sachlichkeit architecture
in both form and planning. Seen as
inherently economic and rational, it was
formally inspired by the Dutch De Stijl
movement, which had important influences
on architecture despite being primarily an
artistic movement.

Walter Gropius, Bauhaus, Dessau, 1926

Rationality

Neue Sachlichkeit architecture was founded on the principle of rationality, that is, of drawing on advances in technology to achieve the greatest architectural effect from the most economic means – a reaction to Expressionism's insistence on personal intuition. In practice the distinction was less stark but apparent, for example, in Taut's shift from vague fantasy to buildings that could actually be realized.

Bruno Taut and Martin Wagner, Britz-Siedlung, Berlin, 1928

Steel, concrete and glass

It was in the mid-1920s buildings of Gropius and Mies, especially (alongside the work of Le Corbusier), that steel, concrete and glass became fully established as the essential materials of Modernist architecture. Gropius's Bauhaus brought these materials' new formal and structural possibilities to the fore, perhaps most dramatically in its cantilevered balconies.

Walter Gropius, Bauhaus, Dessau, 1926

Planar surfaces

The Dutch architect J.J.P. Oud was
appointed chief architect of Rotterdam
in the Netherlands in 1918 and quickly
began to develop a De Stijl-inspired
formal language that was expressive yet
also inherently rational. In his work at
Weissenhofsiedlung he, like many of the
architects involved, made particular use
of planar surfaces to express interior
volumes and to articulate the forms of
individual residences in an otherwise
continuous block.

J.J.P. Oud, 5–9 Weissenhofsiedlung,
Stuttgart, 1927

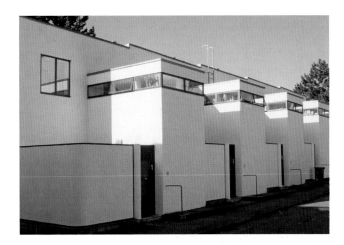

Industrial mass production

New technology and industrial production
enabled the standardization and pre-
fabrication of buildings, especially housing,
as never before. For many, this presented
the possibilities of harnessing technology
towards specific social agendas. Numerous
architects, including Gropius and especially
Ernst May (1886–1970), from 1925 the city
architect of Frankfurt, sought to develop
rationally derived housing prototypes, fit
for the modern age.

Walter Gropius, Torten Estate, Dessau, 1926

Continuous blocks

The building of 'housing', as opposed to
'houses', reflected the socialist agendas
underlying many such projects as
much as their inherent rationality in the
most efficient allocation of resources.
Freestanding Modernist villas were,
in contrast, commonly perceived as a
bourgeois luxury. Despite his work for
the Weissenhofsiedlung, Mies achieved
great success with his designs for the
private house type.

Ludwig Mies van der Rohe, 1–4
Weissenhofsiedlung, Stuttgart, 1927

Region: Initially Europe, later worldwide
Period: 1930s to 1950s
Characteristics: Volume; Steel, concrete and glass; Dematerialization; Free plan; *Piloti;* Universality

Modernism's place on the global stage was cemented in 1932 by Henry-Russell Hitchcock and Philip Johnson's 'Modern Architecture: An International Exhibition' at MoMA. The work of Le Corbusier, Mies, Gropius, Oud and others was shown alongside that by American architects, notably Frank Lloyd Wright and Richard Neutra (1892–1970). All were deemed to be united by a shared Modern Movement aesthetic, with underlying theoretical or social agendas largely glossed over.

Le Corbusier's Purist works of the 1920s played the largest part in defining the International Style. The Villa Savoye at Poissy, France (1928–31), the ultimate embodiment of his 'Five Points' outlined in *Vers une architecture*, stood as the synthesis of his work towards an ideal house type. Earlier examples had included the 'Maison Citrohan' (1922), a mass-produced 'machine for living in', which had appeared in built form at the Weissenhofsiedlung and which was intended to be socially as well as aesthetically transformative. Le Corbusier's ideas extended to the city scale. The 'Ville Contemporaine', exhibited along with the 'Maison Citrohan' at the 1925 Exposition des Arts Décoratifs in Paris, envisaged a new city for 3 million inhabitants composed of rows of multi-use cruciform tower blocks arranged orthogonally. Streets were abolished; cars and pedestrians were separated on different levels. This concept culminated in the deliberately provocative 'Plan Voisin', which envisaged bulldozing half of Paris and replacing it with a 'Ville Contemporaine' orthogonal layout of cruciform blocks. The later, highly influential 'Ville Radieuse' (1935) saw Le Corbusier return

to a more practicable linear plan while retaining the revolutionary character of his earlier ideas.

Mies's work, meanwhile, had begun to evolve from the ascetic Modernism of the Weissenhofsiedlung. His Barcelona Pavilion – formally the German Pavilion at the 1929 International Exposition – distilled Modernism to its cool essential qualities while expanding its palette with exotic marbles and onyx. Containing no space for a dedicated exhibition, the building itself (and its very sparse furnishing, notably Mies's famous 'Barcelona Chair') was intended to evoke the new spirit of Weimar Germany.

Under the spectre of Nazism many architects fled continental Europe. Britain was the destination for Berthold Lubetkin (1901–90), while Gropius, Mendelsohn and Marcel Breuer (1902–81) also passed through, helping to shape the nascent British Modernism before settling in the United States. After closing the Bauhaus in 1933 Mies moved to Chicago where he became director of the architecture school at the Illinois Institute of Technology. This diaspora of architects did much to extend Modernism's influence outside Europe, and ensured a certain international conformity, if not consistency, in style.

Nazism and war had only strengthened the Modernist agendas that had developed in pre-war Europe, and they consequently determined much of the post-war rebuilding programme. Mies's influence in Chicago resulted in the establishment of a corporate Modernism in the United States – arguably the final synthesis of the International Style – exemplified by the work of Hellmuth, Obata + Kassabaum (HOK) and Skidmore, Owings & Merrill (SOM).

Volume

Le Corbusier's early Purist paintings sought to reduce everyday objects to neat formal volumes. This approach consistently informed his architecture, which, in essence, explored the relationship between surface and volume. The Villa Savoye is most perfect expression of this concept: a cuboid volume, split by ribbon windows, floating on *piloti*, with a crowning roof garden above.

Le Corbusier, Villa Savoye, Poissy, France, 1928–31

Steel, concrete and glass

From the mid 1920s steel, concrete and glass became fully established as the essential materials of Modernist architecture. They enabled many of the formal and programmatic innovations that defined the architecture of the International Style. These included a 'free' (unrestricted) plan and façade, demonstrated, for example, at Mies's celebrated Villa Tugendhat.

Ludwig Mies van der Rohe, Villa Tugendhat, Brno, Czech Republic, 1928–30

Dematerialization

The effect of conceiving architecture as the arrangement of a series of volumes, and seeing it realized in steel, concrete and glass, was actually one of dematerialization. The straightforward structural framework allowed the building's skin to be very thin; the wide windows, and the smooth planar surfaces of the walls accentuated the overall effect.

Le Corbusier, Villa Savoye, Poissy, 1928–31

Free plan

One of Le Corbusier's 'Five Points' specified the 'free designing of the ground plan'; as the requirement for internal walls to bear structural loads would be removed, the architect had complete freedom to insert rooms of different sizes within the overall structural frame. Mies's Barcelona Pavilion utilized a wonderfully elegant free plan to create wide open internal spaces, seamlessly blending interior and exterior.

Ludwig Mies van der Rohe, German Pavilion, 1929 Barcelona International Exposition, Spain, reconstruction completed 1986

Piloti

A key feature of Le Corbusier's work in particular, *piloti* – piers or columns that raise a building above ground level – were frequently used to provide space for circulation or storage. At Berthold Lubetkin's Highpoint I, the first coherent example of the International Style in Britain, the whole eight-storey structure is raised up on *piloti*, leaving the ground floor for circulation, storage and communal spaces.

Universality

The intended universality of Le Corbusier's ideas was borne out particularly in the worldwide influence of his theories on urban planning. Following World War II another strand of the International Style evolved into a similarly universal corporate Modernism, through which the architectural language of steel and glass would be found in business districts all over the world.

Berthold Lubetkin, Highpoint I, London, completed 1935

Ludwig Mies van der Rohe and Philip Johnson, Seagram Building, New York City, completed 1958

Region: Europe, especially Germany and Scandinavia
Period: 1930s to 1960s
Characteristics: Techno-fetishism; Radicalism; Local materials; Irregular plan; Fundamentalist forms; Starkness

The notion that function should govern form – or rather that form should follow function in the words of Louis Sullivan's essay of 1896 – was a fundamental tenet of Modernist thinking. Adolf Loos's essay 'Ornament and Crime' (originally published in 1908 but not widely available until it appeared in the review *L'esprit nouveau* in 1920) argued that design was progressing towards the complete elimination of ornament. It was therefore a 'crime' for time and resources to be wasted on what would soon become obsolete.

Following World War I, as Modernists attempted to 'wipe the slate clean', ornament was derided as irrational and nostalgically symbolic of a past age. Although a building's functional requirements determined form as never before, the hand of the architect remained: greater in Expressionism, lesser in the New Objectivity, yet always there. What became known as the International Style emerged as a response to the problem of function generating forms appropriate for the modern age.

Some architects, however, were more unflinchingly radical in their adherence to the functional. Guided by political ideology, in the case of Hannes Meyer (1889–1954), Gropius's successor as Bauhaus director, or by unfailing belief in the transformative potential of technology, in the case of the American Richard Buckminster Fuller (1895–1983), Functionalists rejected the formalism they saw in the International Style. Functionalism arguably took deepest hold in Scandinavia where its two greatest exponents – Arne Jacobsen (1902–71) in Denmark and Alvar Aalto (1898–1976) in Finland – humanized its harsher tendencies.

Although arriving comparatively late, Modernism's underlying social agenda was well received in the social democratic conditions of Sweden and Denmark, while its new aesthetic possibilities were quickly put to work in shaping national identity in Finland, which had become independent only in 1917. The Stockholm Exhibition buildings (1930) by Gunnar Asplund (1885–1940) had introduced the architectural language of steel and glass to Scandinavia, where it was quickly adapted to local traditions and contexts. Jacobsen's Bellavista estate at Klampenborg, Denmark, completed in 1934, alongside his Bellevue Seabath and later theatre, drew from the *Siedlung* prototype but added a rare drama and sense of movement created through its staggered form, a direct response to the beach-side site. Although these works were realized in the white planar forms of the International Style, Jacobsen was soon to widen his range of materials.

Aalto also adapted the elements of the International Style. It was in his Paimio Sanatorium, Finland, begun in 1929, that Aalto set out his principles. The sanatorium's bucolic setting was intended to aid the recuperation of tuberculosis sufferers through exposure to sun and fresh air. Aalto positioned the complex of buildings to maximize light and airflow. For the patients' wing he cantilevered the floors from a concrete spine, allowing internal flexibility and sweeping views of the landscape.

Functionalism continued in the post-war era, but in lesser hands could tend towards the dogmatic and harsh. Hans Scharoun's Berlin Philharmonie (1960–63) was arguably the last great work guided by the Functionalist doctrines developed in the 1920s and 1930s.

Techno-fetishism

Buckminster Fuller's design philosophy was informed by the belief that technology could cure all human ills. His unrealized Dymaxion House (1929) rethought the home for the modern age; it was a bold synthesis of function and technology consisting of a futuristic structure hung from a central mast. He is best known for his geodesic domes such as the Biosphère, originally built for the 1967 World's Fair in Montreal, Canada.

Radicalism

At its core Functionalism was Modernism pushed to its logical limits. Like all radical trends, however, it could veer towards the dogmatic, producing buildings that lacked life and invention. However, when deployed carefully in the right contexts, a Functionalist-informed approach could still yield strikingly dynamic works such as Stirling and Gowan's University of Leicester Engineering Building.

R. Buckminster Fuller, Montreal Biosphère, 1967

Stirling and Gowan, University of Leicester Engineering Building, Leicester, England, 1959–63

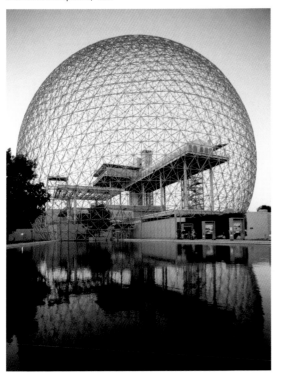

Local materials

The International Style was characterized, at least in its early stages, by its white planar forms, sometimes of rendered brick but most often of concrete. In its Scandinavian variant Functionalism made use of a much wider palette, especially of local materials. Aalto's masterwork, the Villa Mairea, made highly lyrical use of wood; other buildings frequently employed brick and even leather.

Alvar Aalto, Villa Mairea, Noormarkku, Finland, 1938–41

Irregular plan

Functionalists argued that plans should be determined solely by functional requirements; symmetry was unimportant. Their architecture was therefore especially suited to building types that had to serve very specific purposes. Vilhelm Lauritzen laid out the plan of the Broadcasting House in Copenhagen, completed in 1941, according to the specific acoustic requirements of each space, foreshadowing Hans Scharoun's approach in the later Berlin Philharmonie.

Hans Scharoun, Berlin Philharmonie, Berlin, 1960–63

Fundamentalist forms

The forms generated through Functionalism were considered as merely the consequence of the building's spatial requirements. The fundamentalist approach to form is visible in Jacobsen and Erik Møller's Aarhus City Hall. Perhaps influenced by Asplund's Gothenburg City Hall extension of 1936; its form rarely expresses more than its functional requirements, and the clock tower is stripped back to its essential structure.

Arne Jacobsen and Erik Møller,
Aarhus City Hall, Aarhus, Denmark,
inaugurated 1941

Starkness

A consequence of the Functionalists' fundamentalist approach was a starkness that in some instances gave their work a forbidding, almost inhumane character. However, in the hands of Aalto especially – but also in those of others – this starkness took on an essential, poetic quality. This is dramatically apparent in Asplund's extraordinary Skogskyrkogården (Woodland Cemetery) in Stockholm, which has an ethereal calmness and beauty.

Gunnar Asplund, Skogskyrkogården
(Woodland Cemetery), Stockholm, 1917–40

Region: Soviet Union
Period: 1920s to early 1930s
Characteristics: Revolutionary; Abstraction; Industrial buildings; Social programmes; New building types; Traditional construction

If any single project can conjure the extraordinary ambition, yet also the ultimate failure, of the Russian Constructivists, it is Vladimir Tatlin's Monument to the Third International. Designed between 1919 and 1920, Tatlin's Tower – a colossal, spiralling mass of steel – was intended to straddle St. Petersburg's River Neva and to reach 400 metres (1,312 feet) high. Planned as the headquarters of the Third International, or Comintern, the organization charged with forging links between communists internationally and spreading the communist revolution through the world, the Tower was to stand as both a monument to the Russian Revolution and as its 'mouthpiece to the West' (housing the Comintern's administration, the Tower also included a radio transmitter). Fusing art, architecture and industrial engineering, it was intended to be both a functional structure and, through its scale and radical form, a symbol of the new socialist age. That Tatlin's Tower was never built was indicative not only of its unrealistic technological demands, but also the basic shortages of building materials following the Russian Revolution of 1917 and subsequent civil war when architects' work was largely confined to designs on paper.

Constructivism sought the radical fusion of art, industry and technology to create a new visual language for everyday life that would both reflect and further the ideals of the Revolution. Inspired in its form by the theories of the sculptors Naum Gabo and Antoine Pevsner, it initially adopted the abstract geometry of the Suprematist movement in art, already established before the Revolution and best exemplified in the work of the group's leader, Kazimir

Malevich (1878–1935). Artists such as Liubov Popova, Gustav Klutsis and El Lissitzky (1890–1941) began to adapt Suprematism's innovations to create 'constructions' with a strongly three-dimensional spatial character.

In 1920 VKhUTEMAS (Higher State and Artistic and Technical Workshops) was created through the merger of the previously separate art and industrial design schools. VKhUTEMAS, at which Popova, Klutsis and Lissitzky as well as the influential Aleksandr Rodchenko all taught, promoted multi-disciplinary training with wide-ranging topics on space, colour, form and construction. The teaching at VKhUTEMAS had many design applications, from propaganda, typography and set design to photomontage and also architecture.

The architect Aleksandr Vesnin (1883–1959) soon joined the faculty at VKhUTEMAS and with his brothers Leonid (1880–1933) and Victor (1882–1950) became one of the main leaders of Constructivist architecture. Aleksandr and Victor's unrealized design for the newspaper the *Leningrad Pravda* in 1924 can be read as a scaling-up of the propaganda kiosks Klutsis had been developing over the previous few years. In 1925, along with Moisei Ginzburg (1893–1946), the Vesnins founded the OSA group as a Functionalist counterpoint to the formalism that they increasingly detected in the work of other emerging Constructivists. OSA turned its attention to housing and other explicitly multi-use building types intended to break down social hierarchies. These works stand as Constructivism's defining achievements, demonstrative of the unswerving belief in architecture as an instrument of social change.

Revolutionary

Constructivism strived not only to reflect the ideals of the Russian Revolution but to actively promote it. Many artists and architects developed radical forms of agitprop, posters, leaflets and papers, as well as Constructivist kiosks that announced their message through sound and image. The Vesnins' project for Leningrad Pravda combined a traditional newspaper office with a searchlight and revolving billboards in a radically Functionalist building.

Abstraction

The Constructivist rejection of traditional architectural styles was intended to create a *tabula rasa* from which would emerge an authentically revolutionary architecture. While Constructivism was influenced by Suprematism and European varieties of Modernism, it was combined with a hard ideological edge. Melnikov's own house reflects both its insistence on new geometric forms and also the new architecture's adaptability – the diamond-shaped windows were designed to be easily rearranged.

Aleksandr and Victor Vesnin, unrealized project for the *Leningrad Pravda*, 1924

Konstantin Melnikov, Melnikov House, Moscow, 1927–31

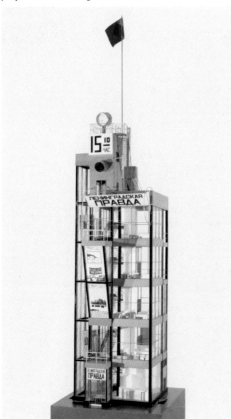

Industrial buildings

State control of the economy resulted in
unprecedented industrial expansion as
Russia moved from a backward agrarian
economy to a modern industrialized state.
Constructivists were engaged in designing
numerous industrial buildings as well as
new factory kitchens to feed the workers
en masse. The latter also fulfilled a key
aspiration of communist ideology of
making it possible for women to work by
liberating them from the domestic sphere.

Aleksandr Vesnin, Nikolai Kolli,
Georgii Orlov, Sergei Andrievskii,
DneproGES, Dam and Hydroelectric
Power Station, Zaporozhye Dnepr
River, Ukraine, 1927–32

Social programmes

Constructivists believed more strongly than any other Modernists in architecture's ability to influence social behaviour. Ginzburg's Narkomfin Communal House is the best known of a number of housing developments in which new modes of communal living were promoted through architecture. There were communal blocks for sleeping, eating, washing and learning, a strategy explicitly aimed towards the breaking down of class structures.

Moisei Ginzburg and Ignatii Milinis, Narkomfin Communal House, Moscow, 1930

New building types

The post-Revolutionary environment necessitated new building types or the radical adaption of existing ones. Workers' clubs were reconfigured to act as 'social condensers', furthering the ideals of the Revolution by bringing people together in new ways. Melnikov designed five clubs in Moscow alone, the Rusakov, with its dynamic cantilevered forms, being the most visually striking.

Konstantin Melnikov, Rusakov Workers' Club, Moscow, 1927

Traditional construction

Although Constructivists aspired to create an architecture that was wholly modern in both aesthetic and construction, they were frequently held back by the widespread lack of modern building technology. Despite its modern form, the Red Banner Textile Factory, begun by Mendelsohn (one of a number of European Modernists, including Le Corbusier, to work in Russia during the 1920s) was actually built using traditional methods.

Erich Mendelsohn, Red Banner Textile Factory, St. Petersburg, 1925–37

Region: Nazi Germany, Fascist Italy, Stalinist Soviet Union
Period: 1930s in Germany and Italy, to 1950s in Soviet Union
Characteristics: Monumental; Anti-avant-garde; Representational; Bombastic classicism; Abstracted classicism; Ritualistic

The totalitarian regimes that emerged in Europe in the 1920s and 1930s in the form of Nazi Germany, Fascist Italy and the Stalinist Soviet Union were characterized by deeply ambiguous relationships with modernity. On the one hand, huge technological and industrial advances allowed the state to extend its reach into everyday life. Yet the social and economic upheavals that resulted from these transformations were seen by many as having suppressed national values and crafts. Visually, this contradiction was most apparent in the varying ways in which architecture was deployed by each regime as an instrument of state power and control.

In its early years the Soviet state had actually fostered numerous and competing avant-garde movements, notably Constructivism. However, as Stalin consolidated his power towards the end of the 1920s, avant-garde art and architecture were suppressed and eventually outlawed as official state styles were established. After Boris Iofan won the competition for the design of the Palace of the Soviets with a stepped classical tower, surmounted by giant statue of Lenin, architecture soon reverted to pre-Revolutionary styles of art and architecture, untainted by Constructivism's perceived Western influence.

The Nazis similarly suppressed Germany's vibrant avant-garde culture once they gained control of the government in 1933. After succeeding Paul Ludwig Troost (1878–1934) as Adolf Hitler's architectural advisor in 1934, Albert Speer (1905–81) immediately set about creating an architecture that would both reflect the perceived unity of the German people and act as a backdrop to the Nazis' expressions of power. Speer's most notable work was arguably the infamous Zeppelinfeld in Nuremberg, the site of numerous fanatical rallies, which fused eclectic classical references with distinctly modern lighting effects. The Nazis' approach to architecture was riddled with contradictions; while Hitler and Speer's plans for reordering Berlin aspired to imitate imperial Rome, in rural contexts Nazi buildings took inspiration from local vernaculars, aiming to channel an 'authentic' German spirit.

In Fascist Italy the situation was more complex, as the avant-garde helped to inform the development of state architecture. Many avowedly Modernist Italian architects were also enthralled by classical architecture, echoing Benito Mussolini's far cruder attempts to create links between his regime and ancient Rome. Marcello Piacentini's buildings for the Sapienza University of Rome during the 1930s involved sophisticated attempts to fuse Modernist and classical forms, an approach that reached its zenith in the Palazzo della Civiltà Italiana, EUR (a residential and business district in Rome), which was intended to commemorate twenty years of Fascism at the aborted 1942 International Exhibition. For the architect Giuseppe Terragni (1904–43), the relationship between Modernism and classical architecture went deeper than equivalent forms. He was closely inspired in particular by Le Corbusier's attempt to distil universal architectural values. Although Terragni's masterwork, the Casa del Fascio, Como, appears Modernist in its apparent objectivity, the ordered repetition of its deliberately open façade reflects a clear affinity with classicism, emphasized by the connection between its inner atrium and piazza outside.

Monumental

Architecture was central to totalitarian regimes' expression of their permanence (despite their obvious novelty). Huge-scale and highly wrought forms, often inspired by the great monuments of antiquity (Speer and Hitler aimed to create a super-sized Pantheon, for example), frequently characterized totalitarian architecture. However, its most enduring monument was Alexei Schushev's relatively small Lenin Mausoleum, which combined abstract Constructivist elements with classical references.

Alexei Schushev, Lenin Mausoleum, Moscow, 1924–30

Anti-avant-garde

Totalitarian regimes were not straight–forwardly anti-Modernist, but were, for the most part, opposed to the avant-garde. Speer's New Chancellery was constructed in vaguely classical forms, though these were abstracted in such a way that would scarcely have been possible before the advent of Modernism. Beyond architecture, this conservatism was not always the rule; the propaganda films of Leni Riefenstahl, notably *Triumph of the Will* (1934), pushed at the boundaries of filmmaking.

Albert Speer, New Chancellery, Berlin, 1938–9

Representational

One criticism of Constructivism was that its rejection of representation made it ill-suited to conveying propaganda messages that a largely uneducated populace could understand. Thus, more conventional forms of representation were reverted to; both Speer and Iofan's pavilions for their respective regimes at the 1937 International Exhibition in Paris made use of figuration – a far cry from Mies's restrained Barcelona Pavilion (see page 164).

Boris Iofan, Russian Pavilion, Paris International Exhibition, 1937

Bombastic classicism

The reversion to 'representational architecture' was most often configured, especially in the Soviet Union, in an overblown, bombastic classicism. Although overtly modern in structure and sheer scale, these buildings were overloaded with classical ornament and figurative sculpture, relying on established and historic modes of architectural hierarchy and legibility in stark contrast to Modernism's supposed *tabula rasa*.

Abstracted classicism

The way totalitarian regimes drew from classicism took many forms. Troost was particularly inspired by Schinkel's stripped-back Neoclassicism, notably in his House of German Art, Munich (completed 1937). In Italy, where the classical legacy was most intense, many architects attempted to fuse a modern sensibility and new building types with abstract classical forms. This is most apparent in the stacked arches of the Palazzo della Civiltà Italiana at EUR, Rome.

Lev Rudnev, Lomonosov University, Moscow, 1947–52

Giovanni Guerrini, Ernesto La Padula and Mario Romano, Palazzo della Civiltà Italiana, EUR, Rome, 1937–42

Ritualistic

For the Zeppelinfeld at Nuremberg Speer
modelled Hitler's speaking platform on
the Pergamon Altar, which had been
housed in Berlin since its excavation in
1879. He combined this feature with huge
searchlights directed vertically into the sky
to create the so-called 'Cathedral of Light',
a visual spectacle so overwhelming that the
Marxist critic Walter Benjamin described
Nazism as the 'aestheticization of politics'.

Albert Speer, 'Cathedral of Light', Zeppelinfeld,
Nuremberg, Germany, 1938

Region: United States
Period: 1910s to 1970s
Characteristics: Spirit; Organic; History; Communality; Abstraction; Monumentality

While most mainstream Modernist thinking regarded the modern age as a *tabula rasa*, other strands of it – which might loosely be termed Essentialist – favoured a focus on the timeless, universal qualities of architecture; the most notable exponents were the American architects Frank Lloyd Wright and Louis Kahn (1901–74).

In 1888 Wright, then in his twenties, began working for Louis Sullivan and was deeply influenced by the latter's attempts to forge an architecture that would embody America's frontier spirit. After leaving Sullivan's office to start his own practice, Wright received numerous commissions for houses in and around Chicago in which he developed and refined his architectural philosophy, culminating with his renowned Prairie Houses, built in the first years of the twentieth century.

Shaped by Wright's quasi-ritualistic view of everyday existence, the Prairie House plans typically radiated out from a central hearth. Other rooms were then arranged loosely around this spiritual centre. Walls and windows were generally downplayed as the interior became a fluid ensemble of intersecting and overlapping spaces. The exteriors, for example at the Ward Willits House (1902), were marked by wide horizontal planes arranged into a kind of stratified system, accentuated by thick overhanging eaves. Each house's spatial rhythm was further refined by the use of particular materials, furnishings and ornamentation as architectural synecdoches; from each component could be extrapolated the essence of the whole.

In the Prairie Houses Wright aspired to meld Arts and Crafts values (and also the influence of traditional Japanese architecture) with the creative possibilities of the machine age, to create modern spaces suitable for the distinctly modern class of people who commissioned them. The apotheosis of this idea was the Usonian House, an inexpensive, largely pre-fabricated, single-storey residence, the design of which was informed by changes in modern lifestyles; there was, for example, no dining room but instead a fluid space uniting kitchen and living areas. The Usonian House was to play a central role in Wright's utopian 'Broadacre City' (1931) plan, which proposed a largely suburban society with an emphasis on nature, enhanced rather than destroyed by modernity – an idea that had particular resonance in the political and economic climate of the New Deal.

Like Wright, for much of his career Louis Kahn stood outside the architectural mainstream and it was only after a stay as architect in residence at the American Academy in Rome during the early 1950s that he arrived at what might be described as his mature style. For Kahn, architecture in its purest sense gave form to the essential meaning underlying each architectural problem. In works such as the Yale University Art Gallery at New Haven, Connecticut, and Richards Medical Research Laboratory, University of Pennsylvania, Kahn evolved an architectural language based on the arrangement of simple geometric forms to convey the meaning of the building's social programme. In his greatest work, the National Assembly Building, Dhaka, Bangladesh, Kahn made the functions of government visible in the plan, and in drawing from old and new, East and West, gave enduring form to the establishment of governmental institutions in a post-colonial state.

Spirit

Wright's Prairie Houses combined many of the traditional elements of his earlier house designs with modern innovations such as open plans and cantilevered roofs, notably at the Robie House. This duality was also represented by their locations on the outskirts of Chicago, between city and frontier, and as both modern and authentically American – ideas furthered in Wright's later, highly influential Usonian (literally 'of the US') house type.

Frank Lloyd Wright, Robie House, South Woodlawn, Chicago, Illinois, 1908–10

Organic

Wright saw architecture as continuous with its surroundings; even his suburban Prairie Houses appear to emerge from the ground. However, it was at Fallingwater, one of his best-known works, where he pushed this idea to its limits. Situated above a ravine, the house features concrete cantilevers that appear to emerge from a central core of local stone, merging interior and exterior to create an almost complete integration of architecture and nature.

Frank Lloyd Wright, Fallingwater, Bear Run, Pennsylvania, 1934–7

History

Both Wright and Kahn had deep yet subtle relationships with history. Kahn's Kimbell Art Museum is vaguely Palladian in plan, while its concrete barrel vaults invite comparison with ancient Roman architecture. Yet Kahn creates a modern spatial tension by using cycloid rather than semicircular geometry in the vault, leaving unexpected, narrow slits at the apexes, which delicately light the open-plan space below.

Louis Kahn, Kimbell Art Museum, Fort Worth, Texas, 1966–72

Communality

The idea of organic architecture was not confined to the relationship of a building to its surroundings but was also key to its programme. Wright's Johnson Wax building in Wisconsin extended the company's approach of treating the organization and its staff like an extended family. Its rich spaces could sustain conversation and collaboration, in practice and in spirit, while retaining a clear expression of corporate hierarchy.

Frank Lloyd Wright, Johnson Wax Administration Centre, Racine, Wisconsin, 1936–9 (tower, 1944–50)

Abstraction

Although there was very little that was Functionalist in either Wright or Kahn's work, they rarely strayed towards pure formalism. Their architectural forms (especially those of Kahn) were generated by abstracting the essence of the architectural problem and the meanings underlying it. Kahn's Yale University Art Gallery, for example, nullifies the variety and confusing styles of the buildings around it with the calm geometric order of its interior.

Louis Kahn, interior of the Yale University Art Gallery, New Haven, Connecticut, 1951–4

Monumentality

Many of Kahn's works are marked by a
monumentality, which is not necessarily
a consequence of their scale but of the
sense that they have a capacity to outlive
the time that conceived them. At Dhaka he
drew on Beaux-Arts planning principles to
create a diagram infused with meanings
related to the building's function and
symbolism. Even after the buildings are
gone, these meanings will still be legible
through the spatial relationships left in the
archaeological record.

Louis Kahn, National Assembly Building,
Dhaka, Bangladesh, 1962–75

Region: Britain
Period: 1950s to 1960s
Characteristics: Sculptural; Raw concrete; Streets in the sky; Urban; Anti-slab; Destruction

Although the term is now frequently used to describe post-war buildings perceived to be 'brutal' in form or materials, Brutalism, as a distinct architectural movement, has a far more specific definition. It centres on the work of the husband-and-wife architect duo Alison (1928–94) and Peter Smithson (1923–2003), who were particularly inspired Le Corbusier's post-war work, notably the Unité d'Habitation in Marseille, France, and buildings in Chandigarh, India; in these buildings the smooth white surfaces of the 1920s and 1930s were superseded by rough expanses of raw concrete, or *béton brut*. Their early Hunstanton School in Norfolk was inspired by Mies's Illinois Institute of Technology buildings in structure and planning, but left the structure and materials deliberately exposed, highlighting the qualities of their crude, apparently unfinished state. The influential critic Reyner Banham dubbed this approach 'the New Brutalism', and argued that leaving materials in an unfinished state as the Smithsons had done constituted an ethical, as much as an aesthetic, proposition.

The defining moment in the emergence and shaping of Brutalism came in 1956 with the seminal 'This is Tomorrow' exhibition at London's Whitechapel Art Gallery. Conceived by the critic Theo Crosby, the exhibition brought together artists and architects with graphic designers and even musicians into 12 collaborative 'groups' that would create work for display. The Smithsons were in the same group as the artist Eduardo Paolozzi and the photographer Nigel Henderson. What in many ways united the various displays was a concern for exploring and representing the city 'as found',

allowing such manifestations of mass culture as the design of advertising, magazines and everyday household items to invigorate the work. These concerns were crystallized in Richard Hamilton's poster design *Just what is it that makes today's homes so different, so appealing?* – a literal assemblage of cut-outs from lifestyle magazines.

Taking London 'as found' in the 1950s also meant dealing with vast swathes of urban landscape that had been ravaged by the Blitz during World War II – in some ways Brutalism's insistence on raw, unarticulated materials can be seen as a response to this aesthetic and emotional experience. The post-war rebuilding programme of housing, hospitals and schools – the architectural manifestation of the new realities of the welfare state – presented obvious opportunities for architects. The urgency of the need for new housing ensured that most initial projects were cheap, quickly constructed 'slab' blocks set in open space. The Smithsons, in contrast, sought to reinvigorate the 'street culture' that they saw as being destroyed by this type of rationalist Modernism. They finally got the chance to put their theories into practice at Robin Hood Gardens, Poplar, London (1966–72). Relatively low-rise compared to contemporary examples, the estate's two buildings were angled around a large inner communal garden, carefully landscaped with raised mounds so that the garden could be enjoyed from even the upper-storey apartments. The blocks, which contained maisonettes as well as single-storey flats, were designed so that the inner arrangement of residences could be read from the outside, which reintroduced a sense of legibility and individuality to an otherwise monolithic Modernism.

Sculptural

Other forms of what might retrospectively
be labelled Brutalism (though distinct from
the strand described as New Brutalism)
exploited concrete's sculptural potential.
The work of Denys Lasdun (1914–2001) was
similarly informed by that of Le Corbusier
but also deeply inspired by the English
Baroque. Buildings such as his Royal
College of Physicians and National Theatre
on the South Bank, both in London, reveal
his ability to connect his highly sculptural
works to their surroundings.

Denys Lasdun, National Theatre,
London, 1967–76

Raw concrete

The defining characteristic of Brutalism –
the one that gave it its name – was its use
of raw concrete, or *béton brut*, inspired by
Le Corbusier's post-war work. This material
gave Brutalist buildings a visceral, almost
elemental, roughness seen also in other
works outside Britain, notably those by Paul
Rudolph (1918–97) in the United States and
Sigurd Lewerentz (1885–1975) in Sweden.

Le Corbusier, La Tourette Monastery,
Éveux-sur-l'Arbresle, near Lyon, France,
1957–60

Streets in the sky

Although unsuccessful, the Smithsons'
entry for the competition to design the
Golden Lane estate in London popularized
the concept of 'streets in the sky'. All
residences would be accessed from decks,
at least partially open to the sky, which it
was hoped would facilitate a 'street culture'
that Modernism had ignored; while on a
more practical level the decks were wide
enough to provide direct access for vehicles
delivering fresh produce.

Jack Lynn and Ivor Smith, Park Hill, Sheffield,
South Yorkshire, 1957–61

Urban

Brutalism aimed to reinstate an urban
culture lost through the Modernist
subjugation of the street and the almost
anti-urban strategy of placing slab blocks
in isolation. The two parts of Robin
Hood Gardens twist and turn, forging
sophisticated relationships with the setting
that is decidedly urban. However, that they
also have to shield their residents from
the city's noise and pollution reveals the
deficiencies of Brutalist urbanism.

Alison and Peter Smithson, Robin Hood
Gardens, Poplar, London, 1966–72

Anti-slab

The Smithsons' Economist Building constituted a rejection of the monolithic slab block and the linear urban strategies of Le Corbusier's 'Ville Radieuse' (1935). They negotiated an irregular, historically sensitive site with three blocks of different heights surrounding a plaza, which enhanced rather than erased the existing urban grain. The result: a building that is bold but not overpowering, polemical yet sympathetic to its context.

Destruction

While Brutalism's strength lay in its radicalism, there was always potential for its polemics to slip into ideological dogmatism; even detailing concrete to mitigate the effects of weathering could be deemed 'immoral'. Thus the few buildings that the Brutalists actually erected have rarely fared well as the political climate and aesthetic sensibilities have evolved. Many Brutalist works are presently in poor condition or have been demolished.

Alison and Peter Smithson,
Economist Building, St. James's,
London, 1959–65

Rodney Gordon for the Owen Luder Partnership,
Trinity Square Car Park, Gateshead, Tyne and Wear,
1962–7, demolished 2010

Region: Japan
Period: 1950s to 1970s
Characteristics: Corbusian influence; Modular; Monumentality; Japanese tradition; Unresolved; Influence

Modernism had arrived in Japan between the world wars. However, it was only when rebuilding began after 1945 that serious discussions took place about how to marry the needs of modernization with deeply entrenched traditional Japanese values.

Kenzo Tange (1913–2005), the leader of these debates, was deeply inspired by Le Corbusier and had been a pupil of the pioneer Japanese Modernist Kunio Maekawa (1905–86), who had actually worked with the great master in Paris in the late 1920s. Tange's first significant project, the Peace and Memorial Museum, Hiroshima, comprised a long, thin rectangular building raised up on *piloti*, its elevation calmly articulated with repeating vertical fins, all composed from rough, unfinished concrete. A monument in the form of a hyperbolic paraboloid arch (hinting at Tange's later Yoyogi National Gymnasium) created an axis between Tange's museum and the surviving 'A-Bomb Dome' across the river.

The museum building itself was clearly inspired by Le Corbusier's 'Five Points', while his work at Chandigarh in the 1950s informed its raw forms and monumental planning. Yet the whole project remained deeply connected to traditional Japanese construction and spatial principles. The Corbusian concrete frame, which negated the need for supporting interior walls, had close parallels with Japanese timber-frame construction that allowed a free interior arrangement with (often moveable) screens. Fluidity between interior and exterior, created by sliding doors and windows, was fundamental to both Modernism and traditional Japanese building; even the standardization of forms and materials, one of Modernism's chief innovations, was argued to have

Japanese equivalents. Thus in many ways Tange's whole Hiroshima project represented the merging of Modernism with local tradition and contexts to develop a new kind of monumentality.

In 1960 Japanese Modernism gained international attention at the World Design Conference held in Tokyo. Under the guidance of Tange and partly influenced by the ideas of the radical Team X, a group of mainly young architects who had challenged mainstream Modernist thinking, several architects, including Kisho Kurokawa (1934–2007), Kiyonori Kikutake (1928–2011) and Fumihiko Maki (b. 1928), published a pamphlet entitled *Metabolism 1960: Proposals for a New Urbanism*, which advocated the fusion of technologist Modernism with Buddhist notions of fluidity and impermanence. The ideas of the Metabolists, as they were known, extended from the single building to the city scale. Architecture, they argued, should be changeable, dynamic and akin to a cell capable of undergoing metabolic transformation. Reflecting the huge economic and social changes Japan was then experiencing, the Metabolists regarded technology as having the potential to inform how cities developed; like Britain's Archigram group, they produced numerous schemes for modular cities loosely conceived as organisms, with pods that could be inserted in and taken out as technology progressed.

Although Metabolism could be read as anti-form, it did not entirely reject monumentalism. In a similar way to several of Arata Isozaki's city schemes, Tange's Yamanashi Press and Broadcasting Centre, with its concrete cylinders and studios and the offices suspended between, signified both adaptability and a latent monumentality.

Corbusian influence

Le Corbusier's work in Chandigarh –
both the overall urban plan and several
administrative buildings for the new
capital city of Haryana and Punjab states
– demonstrated how Modernism could be
adapted to local contexts. It provided an
important model for interpreting Modernist
strictures and finding resonances between
international Modernism and native
traditions and contexts.

Kenzo Tange, Peace and Memorial Museum,
Hiroshima, 1949–55

Modular

The Metabolists conceived a building as a kind of synthesis of organism and machine. Like a cell, the building comprised a collection of semi-autonomous components; however, these could be replaced as needed in a similar way to the parts of a machine. This idea was realized most notably in Kurokawa's Nakagin Capsule Tower, which is composed of more than 100 self-contained replaceable pods.

Monumentality

Despite the Metabolists' interest in notions of impermanence, many of their works aspired to monumentality. This could be attributed to their frequent use of raw concrete in place of the timber-frame construction of traditional Japanese architecture. However, it was also a characteristic of the boldness of their designs, such as the radical roof form of Tange's Yoyogi National Gymnasium, built for the 1964 Olympic Games in Tokyo.

Kisho Kurokawa, Nakagin Capsule Tower, Tokyo, 1972

Kenzo Tange, Yoyogi National Gymnasium, Tokyo, 1961–4

Japanese tradition

Reflecting various strands of Buddhist thinking, traditional Japanese architecture made almost exclusive use of wood, with inner spaces divided by moveable screens and little distinction between interior and exterior. The notions of impermanence and fluidity inherent in it were highly important for the Metabolists' technology-infused visions.

Kiyonori Kikutake, Sky House, Tokyo, 1959

Unresolved

Metabolist architecture was inherently unresolved. That is to say that a Metabolist building was never finished but it was always deliberately left open to be added to and modified. This extended to the city scale with Tange's 'A Plan for Tokyo 1960', the best known of a number of urban schemes drawn up by the Metabolists that were entirely modular, negating established notions of centre and periphery.

Kenzo Tange, Yamanashi Press and Broadcasting Centre, Kofu, 1961–7

Influence

Although it responded to specifically Japanese cultural and economic conditions, the Metabolists' work proved influential beyond Japan. Their ideas pre-empted the widespread collapse of distinctions between public and private spheres in the West, heralded by new technology such as the Sony Walkman (a portable audio cassette player). While younger architects such as Arata Isozaki (b. 1931) have moved away from Metabolism's overt technologism towards more elemental concerns, Japanese architecture retains an international prominence.

Arata Isozaki, new entrance for Caixa Forum, Barcelona, Spain, 1999–2002

Region: International
Period: 1970s to 1980s
Characteristics: Technophilia; Industrial aesthetic; Exterior services; Innovative circulation; Wide-span interior spaces; Exposed structure

High-Tech burst forth in 1977 with the completion of the radical Centre Georges Pompidou in Paris, designed by the young team of Richard Rogers (b. 1933) and Renzo Piano (b. 1937). Part museum, part arts centre, the Pompidou aimed to make cutting-edge art accessible to all. The building's innovation was to turn its insides out (hence the term 'bowelism' used by the influential critic Reyner Banham to describe an early iteration of what would become High-Tech). Services (which were colour-coded), circulation space (including lifts and escalators) and above all the building's very structure were moved to its exterior, leaving the interior space unencumbered by supporting columns and so, it was hoped, almost infinitely flexible.

On the one hand High-Tech could be seen as the logical conclusion of the Modernist precept that form should follow function; form was entirely determined by the requirements of the interior space and was therefore almost aggressively direct in its visual assault. Yet on the other High-Tech could, at its core, be seen as explicitly anti-form, barely acknowledging its existence as an architectural idea: the physical manifestation of a building was simply a by-product of its programme. High-Tech had several antecedents, perhaps most notably in the work of the Archigram group based at London's Architectural Association School of Architecture in the mid 1960s. Archigram's seductive,

graphic design-inspired imagery – such as Peter Cook's 'Plug-in City', which imagined a city as a kind of organism to which cell-like components could be added in the absence of autonomous buildings – emphasized adaptability and expendability; components could be swapped as technology progressed. Other architect–thinkers outside Archigram, such as the maverick Cedric Price (1934–2003), were more specifically concerned with technology's potential for driving social and political transformations: Price's unrealized 'Fun Palace', conceived with theatre director Joan Littlewood in 1961 as a social space, aimed at blurring conventional notions of performance and participation.

Despite its iconoclastic zeal and, in some hands, foundation in the idea of social transformation, High-Tech has ironically become best known for its commercial and corporate applications. Many early High-Tech works, notably those by Nicholas Grimshaw (b. 1939) and Michael Hopkins (b. 1935), were industrial or scientific buildings with which the style had a natural affinity. The two most famous works of High-Tech after the Pompidou, however, are office buildings: Rogers's Lloyd's Building in London and Norman Foster's HSBC Main Building in Hong Kong; High-Tech's wide-span interior spaces, which characterized the Pompidou, also proved particularly suited to commercial trading floors.

Technophilia

What made High-Tech Modernist as opposed to Postmodernist was its core belief in the fundamental potential of technology to enable social change. Influenced by the writings of the critic Reyner Banham, High-Tech's technophilia sought to set architecture – and its users – free from form and tradition. Rogers's Lloyd's Building is frequently described as being like an oil rig in the blunt display of its building technology.

Industrial aesthetic

Because of its technophilia, High-Tech was characterized by a strongly industrial aesthetic. This, along with its inherent flexibility, meant that it was readily applied to industrial buildings, such as the early Reliance Controls factory, Swindon, Wiltshire (1967), by Team 4 (Rogers and Foster's short-lived practice) and Grimshaw's Financial Times Printworks in London.

Richard Rogers Partnership, Lloyd's Building, London, 1978–84

Grimshaw Architects, Financial Times Printworks, Docklands, London, completed 1988

Exterior services

To facilitate the flexibility of the interior,
High-Tech architects removed structural
articulation and services to the building's
exterior. Here, along with the typical steel
frame, elements such as pipes, ducts
and vents became part of the building's
aesthetic statement: the logical visual
expression of the requirements of the brief.

Richard Rogers and Renzo Piano,
Centre Georges Pompidou (exterior),
Paris, completed 1977

Innovative circulation

Locating the lifts (elevators) and escalators on the exterior of the Pompidou freed up its interior spaces and also made navigation in the building simpler and more efficient. Foster took a similar approach for the HSBC Main Building in Hong Kong, creating external lifts and providing a huge internal atrium to facilitate social interaction among employees.

Foster + Partners, HSBC Main Building, Hong Kong, completed 1985

Wide-span interior spaces

Sophisticated engineering allowed early High-Tech architects to create wide-span interior spaces, uninterrupted by supporting piers and thus with a completely flexible layout. This characteristic attracted the interest of numerous commercial clients looking to create huge, continuous trading floors.

Richard Rogers and Renzo Piano, Centre Georges Pompidou (interior), Paris, completed 1977

Exposed structure

In Norman Foster's Sainsbury Centre at the University of East Anglia, the otherwise plain, cuboidal form is enlivened by the steel space-frame structure. The steel structure creates a mediating zone outside the internal art gallery space, containing the building's services and serving also to help regulate light and other environ-mental conditions fundamental to the gallery's function.

Foster + Partners, Sainsbury Centre for Visual Arts, University of East Anglia, Norwich, Norfolk, opened 1978

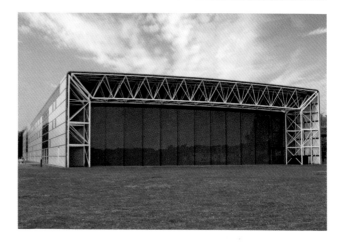

After Modernism

'Modern architecture died in St. Louis, Missouri, on July 15, 1972, at 3.32pm (or thereabouts).' So declared the critic and landscape architect Charles Jencks in the opening to his book *The Language of Post-Modern Architecture* (1977). The apparently epoch-defining event to which Jencks referred was the destruction of Minoru Yamasaki's Pruitt–Igoe housing development. Fully complete in 1956, Pruitt–Igoe's 33 blocks, 11 storeys high, lasted less than 20 years. By the end they had become infamous for violence, poverty and decay, receiving, as Jencks wrote, the 'final coup de grâce by dynamite'.

The Death and Life of Great American Cities

Pruitt–Igoe became symbolic of what was by then a familiar tale of the unintended consequences of Modernist architecture. Modernism was increasingly seen as exacerbating the atomization of industrial societies that it was intended to alleviate. Inevitably the situation was more complex at Pruitt–Igoe, as much as it was elsewhere. While the United States government had paid for Pruitt–Igoe's construction, running costs were to be collected from tenants' rents, but because they were poor, the income was never sufficient and blocks were poorly maintained. The development's completion had coincided with a collapse in St. Louis's urban population as its affluent white communities fled to the suburbs, taking jobs and industry with them. Little prospect of work remained for Pruitt–Igoe's mostly black residents, who were thus forced to live under a draconian welfare regime. Despite these mitigating factors Pruitt–Igoe was a resounding confirmation that Modernism's insistence on architecture as an instrument of change was misguided. Modernism was in any case already under vocal attack, notably from writer and activist Jane Jacobs, whose *The Death and Life of Great American Cities* (1961) offered a stinging rebuke to Modernist urban planning.

'Grand narratives' overturned

The constant attacks directed at Modernist architecture during the 1960s and 1970s reflected much broader critiques of Enlightenment notions of progress and of 'grand narratives', of which Modernism was among the most visible. Neo-liberal economics, concomitant deindustrialization and the emergence of service-based 'knowledge economies' appeared to render irrelevant Marx's prediction of the emancipation of the specifically industrial working class. The French philosopher Jean-François Lyotard was one of the more influential to articulate what he called *The Postmodern Condition* (the title of his 1979 book): 'In contemporary society and culture – postindustrial society, postmodern culture … the grand narrative has lost its credibility, regardless of what mode of unification it uses, regardless of whether it is a speculative narrative or a narrative of emancipation.' In architecture, this line of thought thereby rejected the idea of any form of meta-framework, Modernist or otherwise, that gave a building a broader purpose or meaning beyond that which it contained intrinsically – everything became relative.

One of the main criticisms of Lyotard was that his repudiation of grand narratives was itself a grand narrative. Moreover, identifying Modernist architecture solely in this way belied its huge formal, spatial and structural variety, especially as it began to respond to local traditions and contexts. Nevertheless, Lyotard's (and others') arguments gained currency, and their advocacy of multiple small narratives or discourses to replace the monolithic grand narrative provided an interesting direction in which architecture could go structurally, if not in content.

Initially, architecture veered towards the symbolic 'language games' of Postmodernism that Jencks championed; the ironical use of classical ornamentation was an overtly representational counterpoint to Modernism's instrumentality. Postmodernism was, however, ultimately a short-lived, reactionary phenomenon and from the 1980s there has been an extraordinary diversity in architectural expression and approach. The rise of computer modelling has allowed new and radical possibilities for architectural form and for analysing building performance, with sustainability now a guiding principle for architects of all persuasions.

Regionalism

Postmodernism

Deconstructivism

Eco-architecture

**Expressive
Rationalism**

Contextualism

Region: International
Period: 1960s to present
Characteristics: Inventive forms; Mood; Climate; Identity; Local typologies; Purity

As soon as Modernism began to be exported and taken up outside Europe in the 1930s, its goal of universalization met the particularities of varying local traditions and climates. Indeed, even in Europe Modernism was quickly adapted to local conditions, especially in and around the Mediterranean. Josep Lluís Sert (1902–83) was the most notable of a group of Spanish architects who married Corbusian Modernist principles with traditional devices and materials. The Casa Malaparte, Capri, Italy (1928–42), by Adalberto Libera (1903–63) and his client, Curzio Malaparte, was recognizably Modernist, but adapted its forms to its singular situation, perched on a rocky outcrop high above the sea. It was an elegant response to the fundamental questions of context and topography, ones that Le Corbusier himself faced on a much larger scale in several urban projects for Algiers in the 1930s.

As many Modernist architects fled Europe after the rise of totalitarian regimes in the 1930s, their ideas went with them. Erich Mendelsohn's work in Israel in the 1930s was among the most notable. Some countries meanwhile had already begun to develop and sustain their own Modernist cultures, especially Brazil; there in his design for the new capital of Brasília Oscar Niemeyer (1907–2012) drew from Brazil's landscape – its mountains, rivers and beaches – to create an architectural language of curving forms and volumes. Lúcio Costa (1902–98), who designed the plan for the new capital, was inspired by Le Corbusier's 'Ville Radieuse' and situated Niemeyer's buildings in open ground, accentuating their peculiarly Brazilian modern monumentality.

As the 1960s and 1970s progressed architects began to turn away from Modernism as a universal guiding principle. Globalization and mass migration to cities, in developing countries especially, posed existential threats to traditional cultures and values; while the proliferation of steel-and-glass skyscrapers – a kind of corporate Modernism – led to an increasingly international architectural homogeneity. Architects in many different cultures and climates began to move beyond the apparent constraints of Modernism to embrace local materials, typologies and vernaculars. In some instances this resulted in facile and superficial 'veneerism', but in others architects sensitively absorbed and abstracted the issues posed by tradition, context and climate to form a reconstituted, specifically regional Modernism attuned to local identities – what the critic Kenneth Frampton in an essay of 1983 termed 'Critical Regionalism', describing an approach that had already been happening for several decades.

Inventive forms

Post-war Latin American Modernism was
marked by bold forms and structures,
including large cantilevers, parabolic
vaults and concrete shells. Often architects
were inspired by local vernaculars or even
ancient ruins; in Brasília it was the absence
of such precedent that allowed Niemeyer to
develop a language of monumental curving
forms, vividly realized in the Plaza of the
Three Powers.

Oscar Niemeyer, Plaza of the Three Powers,
Brasília, Brazil, 1958

Mood

Drawing inspiration from Surrealism as
well as contemporary Mexican abstract
geometric painting, Luis Barragán
(1902–88) utilized planes of colour, light
and water to create spaces of a poetic,
almost transcendental quality, yet of a
distinctly Mexican mood. Fellow Mexicans
Ricardo Legorreta (1931–2011) and Teodoro
González de León (b. 1926) followed this
approach, mirroring, albeit in a quite
different context, concerns of the Japanese
architect Tadao Ando.

Luis Barragán, Casa Barragán, Tacubaya,
Mexico City, Mexico, 1947

Climate

In Australia, Harry Seidler (1923–2003)
designed firmly in the International Style,
although his works of the 1950s and 1960s
did incorporate some concessions to
climate and the vernacular. A generation
later Glenn Murcutt (b. 1936) reconfigured
Australian Modernism to create a number
of houses that looked towards the
corrugated iron sheds of the 'outback'
vernacular as well as Aboriginal
shelters. Inextricably linked to their
settings, they made poetic use of natural
light and ventilation.

Glenn Murcutt, Ball-Eastaway House, Glenorie,
New South Wales, Australia, 1980–83

Identity

The historicism of Western Postmodernism
was usually manifested superficially
or ironically. However, a sincere
understanding of contexts, and their
social, political and religious histories,
could inform a new architecture reflecting
local values. Geoffrey Bawa's Sri Lankan
Parliament Building symbolized the
complex religious and racial diversity of
the post-colonial state through the image
of a scaled-up village meeting house.

Geoffrey Bawa, Parliament Building,
Colombo, Sri Lanka, 1980–83

Local typologies

The creative adaptation of local typologies is a frequent characteristic of Regionalism. Ernesto Rogers's Torre Velasca (1956–8) in Milan, Italy, an early example, intriguingly adapted an Italian castle tower form to modern use and scale. In his Asian Games Housing, New Delhi, Raj Rewal (b. 1934) rejected the Modernist slab in favour of a low-rise solution with irregular forms, narrow streets and courtyards following local vernaculars.

Raj Rewal, Asian Games Housing, New Delhi, India, 1980–82

Purity

Eduardo Souto de Moura (b. 1952), like his teacher, Álvaro Siza (b. 1933), produces work that emerges from a profound reading of the patterns and poetics of place. Built into the side of a quarry, the two sides of the Estádio Municipal de Braga are defined by their material and formal purity, invoking notions of local identity and memory – a far cry from most contemporary stadia.

Eduardo Souto de Moura, Estádio Municipal de Braga, Braga, Portugal, 2003

Region: International, especially in the United States and Britain
Period: 1970s to early 1990s
Characteristics: Fragmentation; Architecture as image; Complexity; Contradiction; 'Camp'; Veneer-ism

In 1966 Robert Venturi (b. 1925) published his now seminal book *Complexity and Contradiction in Architecture*. Part manifesto, part architectural scrapbook accumulated over the previous decade, the book represented a *Vers une architecture* (see page 148) for a new generation of architects who had grown up with Modernism but who felt increasingly constrained by its perceived rigidities. Invoking precedents as varied as Borromini, Lutyens and Aalto, Venturi advocated an architecture of quotation, fragments and multiple layers, all brimming with symbolism and meaning. In many respects the Modernism that Venturi railed against was a contrived, caricatured version, embodied by steel-and-glass corporate Modernism and the large-scale urban interventions of the 1960s that often bisected city centres with huge motorways. Despite the fact that both these examples were, of course, a far cry from true Modernist ideals, eclecticism and ambiguity were to be embraced and celebrated as an antidote to Modernism's perceived overbearing blandness.

Venturi's work reflected the broader counter-cultural mood of the 1960s which saw younger generations begin to question and challenge the political, social and racial realities with which they found themselves confronted. Venturi's coining of 'less is a bore' to parody Mies's well-known maxim 'less is more' was highly symbolic of the era's wider challenges to authority. Pop Art, especially the painters Andy Warhol, Robert Rauschenberg and Jasper Johns, subverted the quasi-spiritual formalism of Abstract Expressionism by drawing from the iconography and mass production of popular culture. The Bavinger House (1950) in Norman, Oklahoma, by Bruce Goff (1904–82), which claimed a wide variety of sources and incorporated natural materials and *objets trouvés* (found objects) into its structure, constituted the almost precise architectural equivalent. Similarly eschewing Modernism's social and technological agendas, Venturi called for the humble street – 'Main Street is almost all right' – to be celebrated for its inherent complexity, both for its forms and the types of cultures and social relationships it sustained, an argument that mirrored the similarly widely read work of Jane Jacobs. The *ne plus ultra* of Postmodern culture was, of course, the city of Las Vegas, Nevada, which Venturi along with his wife and business partner, Denise Scott Brown (b. 1931), and Steven Izenour (1940–2001) celebrated in their book, *Learning from Las Vegas* (1972), as the natural expression of everyday America.

Whatever radical edge Post–modernism had originally possessed was firmly blunted by the 1980s. The explosion of the financial services industries in the United States and Britain drove a boom in office towers adorned with classical mouldings – a glib riposte by these new upstarts to the dour older city institutions.

Fragmentation

The Städtisches Museum, designed
by Hans Hollein (b. 1934), stands in
stark contrast to the megastructures of
Archigram and of the Metabolists
(see page 186), arguably the last gasps
of monolithic conceptions of the city.
Separated out over the site, its fragmented
structure allows the building to operate
at different scales through a variety of
formal strategies and the use of a range
of materials.

Hans Hollein, Städtisches Museum,
Mönchengladbach, Germany, 1972–82

Architecture as image

Learning from Las Vegas made the now renowned distinction between the 'duck' and the 'decorated shed'. The former was identified with Modernism and involved a suppression of the building's programme in favour of its overall symbolic expression. In the latter the programme was entirely detached from the building's role in communicating meaning through ornament, freeing its imagistic potential.

Robert Venturi, Vanna Venturi House, Chestnut Hill, Philadelphia, 1963

Complexity

While the 1960s saw Venturi embrace classicism, the so-called New York Five of Peter Eisenman (b. 1932), Richard Meier (b. 1934), Charles Gwathmey (1938–2009), John Hejduk (1929–2000) and Michael Graves (b. 1934) resorted to an avowedly formalist Modernism. While Graves did eventually turn to classicism, his Benacerraf House alludes to the type of formal complexities that his cohort would later develop.

Michael Graves, addition to Benacerraf House, Princeton, New Jersey, 1969

Contradiction

Sitting alongside the symmetrically winged old museum, the Neue Staatsgalerie by James Stirling (1926–92) deployed monumental curving forms and overt classical references, conjuring the spirit of the ruined Roman Forum, yet also featured High-Tech glazing and garish colour. For its architect the Staatsgalerie was 'representation *and* abstract, monumental *and* informal, traditional *and* high tech'.

James Stirling with Michael Wilford, Neue Staatsgalerie, Stuttgart, Germany, 1977–84

'Camp'

In 1964 the critic Susan Sontag described 'camp' as the sensibility that emphasized 'texture, sensuous surface, and style at the expense of content … [that revelled in] the exaggerated, the "off", of things-being-what-they-are-not … [and that] sees everything in quotation marks'. Postmodernism's staginess, artifice and often glossy sensuality meant that it often verged towards an architectural manifestation of this sensibility.

Charles Moore, Piazza d'Italia, New Orleans, 1975–9

Veneer-ism

In office architecture especially Postmodernism was only skin deep; the underlying structure was usually very similar, if not identical, to that of Modernist buildings. While essentially Modernist in structure, Philip Johnson's AT&T Building was topped with a broken pediment apparently inspired by eighteenth-century furniture by Thomas Chippendale, while its three-part vertical division recalled Sullivan's Chicago towers of the 1890s (see page 151).

Philip Johnson, AT&T Building, New York, 1981–4

Region: International
Period: 1980s to early 1990s
Characteristics: Layering; Metaphor; Fragmentation; Sculptural; Intertextuality; Flowing curves

Architecture and literary theory have always had an uneasy relationship. Following World War II the idea that architecture was a language – that its forms and structure could convey meaning in the same way as letters and words, and that it could therefore be made to conform to grammatical principles – was explored by architectural theorists as well as those outside the discipline, notably the Italian writer Umberto Eco. Structuralist linguistic theory, as mediated through the writings of the French anthropologist Claude Lévi-Strauss, informed the work of a number of architects during the 1960s and 1970s including Ralph Erskine (1914–2005) and Aldo van Eyck (1918–99). However, it was arguably only during the 1980s with the shift towards Post-Structuralism that synergies between architecture and various linguistic models began to be seriously sought.

The exhibition 'Deconstructivist Architecture' at New York's Museum of Modern Art in 1988, organized by Philip Johnson and Mark Wigley, attempted to make explicit the links between architecture and Deconstruction, the particular brand of Post-Structuralist linguistics associated with the French philosopher Jacques Derrida. Deconstruction constituted a broad-based critique of Western philosophy and the overturning of the binary oppositions that Derrida saw as governing it. Derrida attempted to subvert the in-built hierarchy of this system – encapsulated by the tyranny of 'signified' over 'signifier' – with new terms and concepts, notably *différance*, that evaded binary opposition.

For architects Deconstruction offered a way of evading the binary oppositions that up to that point had defined architecture: order/disorder, function/form, rationality/expression and, most pressingly during the 1970s and 1980s, Modernism/Postmodernism. Applied to built form, for example in the work of Frank Gehry (b. 1929), Peter Eisenman or Daniel Libeskind (b. 1946), who all featured in the MoMA show, Deconstruction was manifested through fragmented abstract forms, bricolage, and complex relationships to context and site.

The exhibition title's ungainly assimilation of the words Deconstruction and Constructivism alluded to the influence that Russian Constructivism had begun to exert on architects such as Zaha Hadid (b. 1950), Rem Koolhaas (b. 1944), Bernard Tschumi (b. 1944) and Austrian practice Coop Himmelb(l)au, the other architects represented in the show. This Constructivist link was appropriate in a further way, because many Deconstructivist projects were similarly confined to paper. However, seemingly exponential increases in computing power allowed the previously unbuildable to be realized, while since the 1980s architects have also moved away from the literary underpinnings of Deconstructivism. Today computer-based architectural modelling using technology imported from car and aviation design allows design parameters to be altered in real time, a development that has led Zaha Hadid's practice partner Patrik Schumacher to coin Parametricism as the name for a new, all-encompassing style deriving from the use of these technologies.

Layering

Although in many respects Richard Meier
has continued the neo-Modernist project
of the New York Five, his multi-layered
buildings of the 1980s shared many
characteristics with Deconstructivism.
The dynamic layering of quotations from
Le Corbusier's villas, especially in his
Museum für Kunsthandwerk in Frankfurt,
allows the building to forge complex
relationships to the different scales of
its surroundings.

Metaphor

The complex geometry of Daniel
Libeskind's Jewish Museum in Berlin
was partly iconographic, representing an
abstract Star of David, and partly indexical,
with axes radiating to addresses of Jewish
families murdered in the Holocaust.
The structure itself is lit by wound-like
openings, which perforate its envelope
and the various routes mapped into it – an
extraordinary and haunting reflection on
Jewish civilization and the Nazis' attempts
to destroy it in the Holocaust.

Richard Meier, Museum für Kunsthandwerk,
Frankfurt, Germany, 1981–5

Daniel Libeskind, Jewish Museum,
Berlin, 1989–96

Fragmentation

Although he shied away from the
description, Frank Gehry's Guggenheim
Museum in Bilbao is by far the best-known
building associated with Deconstructivism.
Designed using both conventional models
and computer software developed for
Mirage fighter jets, the Guggenheim's
complex fragmented forms of reflective
titanium resulted in the building becoming
an instant global architectural icon.

Frank Gehry, Guggenheim Museum,
Bilbao, Spain, opened 1997

Sculptural

Commissioned by President François Mitterrand as a distinctly twenty-first-century landscape park, Bernard Tschumi's Parc de la Villette contained a number of red-steel follies providing points of focus. Recalling sculpture by Anthony Caro (in particular his *Early One Morning*, 1962) and Constructivist agitprop structures, the follies' forms were determined according to an arbitrary system with the intention that they have no fixed referent.

Bernard Tschumi, Parc de la Villette, Paris, 1982–93

Intertextuality

The Post-Structuralist theorist Julia Kristeva's notion of intertextuality – the way in which one text's meaning is shaped by other texts – has synergies with the work of Peter Eisenman. His Wexner Center alternates between the mismatched grids of the existing university campus, combining sliced and splayed, vaguely castellated forms with bare steel structures to move beyond ideas of function and context.

Peter Eisenman, Wexner Center for the Visual Arts, University of Ohio, Athens, Ohio, 1990

Flowing curves

Although she was a key participant in the 1988 MoMA exhibition, Zaha Hadid had built nothing up until that point. However, since then she has emerged as one of the most celebrated global architects, and has realized projects on several continents. Assisted by the advances of parametric design, Hadid's work is now characterized by flowing curves and internal spaces barely conceivable even 20 years ago.

Zaha Hadid, MAXXI – National Museum of the 21st Century Arts, Rome, opened 2010

Region: International
Period: 1970s to present
Characteristics: On-site energy generation; Green roof; Traditional materials; Adaptation of local forms; New technology; Beyond architecture

Sustainability – the minimizing of a building's impact on the environment during construction and over its lifetime – has the potential to become a new organizing principle for architecture, akin to a new Modernism. Powered by fossil fuels – first coal, now oil and gas – modern industry has made possible the greatest period of development in human history, but it has caused unprecedented environmental destruction and pollution on both a local and, increasingly, a planet-wide scale.

Aligned to the transformative potential of technology and industrial production, Modernism was little interested in the environmental implications of modernity. Even Frank Lloyd Wright's 'organic architecture', exemplified in the seminal Fallingwater house (1934–7; see page 179), made extensive use of environmentally deleterious reinforced concrete for its dramatic cantilevered 'trays'. Even with the use of *brises-soleil*, Modernism's archetypal steel-and-glass structures performed very poorly environmentally and usually required air conditioning (a necessity for skyscrapers) to maintain reasonable living and working conditions. Furthermore Modernist city planning was generally designed around the emancipating possibilities of the private car with little concern for its polluting side-effects.

The rise of the environmental movement in the 1960s coincided with, and in some ways echoed, numerous critiques of Modernism. Rachel Carson's influential *Silent Spring* (1962) is widely seen as providing an important stimulus for environmentalism. In the book Carson outlined how DDT, a pesticide used extensively against mosquitoes with the intention of eradicating malaria, was having unforeseen harmful effects on birds – and potentially humans too – as it moved up the food chain. In many ways, this example embodied the paradox of Modernism; despite the best intentions of architects and planners, their ideas often had unintended and damaging consequences on both people and the environment.

The widely reproduced 'Earthrise' photograph taken by the astronaut William Anders, while in lunar orbit on the Apollo 8 mission in 1968, revealed the limits and fragility of the Earth. This was reflected in James Lovelock's influential, yet still controversial 'Gaia' theory, first published in 1979, that saw the Earth as single organism with all its elements operating in careful balance. As the 1980s and 1990s progressed environmentalism gained further ground as concerns broadened from nuclear power and weapons and ozone-layer depletion to include deforestation and climate change – all with numerous and complex architectural implications.

Increasingly architects are assimilating the lessons of pre-modern vernacular architecture in which buildings were constructed with local materials and adapted according to local environmental conditions. Meanwhile complex computer modelling allows buildings' potential environmental performance to be analyzed and improved during the design stage. In this sense, as a building's environmental performance is increasing factored into its design, the notion of sustainability widens the scope of architecture's social, political and economic role, and gives architects new moral imperatives for their work.

On-site energy generation

Buildings are always consuming energy, be it through lighting, heating or ventilation. Generating energy on-site can often be more efficient (and cheaper) than relying on national energy grids. Solar panels, wind turbines or ground source heat pumps can be retrofitted to existing buildings as well as included in new ones; the solar panels on the Kaohsiung National Stadium by Toyo Ito (b. 1941) are incorporated into its sinuous, futuristic structure.

Toyo Ito, Kaohsiung National Stadium, Kaohsiung, Taiwan, completed 2009

Green roof

Found frequently in vernacular architecture all over the world, green roofs are increasingly part of the standard vocabulary for sustainable architecture. They provide good insulation, absorb rainwater (especially important in urban environments) and can even create habitats for certain types of wildlife. The Singaporean practice WOHA in particular has expanded the concept to integrate gardens, some with trees, in many of its buildings.

WOHA, Iluma (Shopping Centre and Cinema), Singapore, completed 2009

Traditional materials

The manufacture of concrete contributes in the region of 5 per cent of man-made carbon dioxide emissions per year. Using sustainable, locally sourced materials can therefore massively reduce a building's environmental impact. For their Downland Gridshell, sustainability pioneers Edward Cullinan Architects used green oak to create an innovative grid frame, which embodies a minute fraction of the energy of an equivalent steel structure.

Edward Cullinan Architects, Downland Gridshell, Weald & Downland Museum, Sussex, England, 1996–20027

Adaptation of local forms

Renzo Piano's Jean-Marie Tjibaou Cultural Centre, named after the leader of the Kanak independence movement, was built to celebrate local Kanak culture and to present it to the world. Its soaring 'sails', based on conical Kanak buildings, are realized in local iroko timber, creating a complex set of buildings in tune with the local climate and natural landscape.

Renzo Piano, Jean-Marie Tjibaou Cultural Centre, Nouméa, New Caledonia, South Pacific, 1991–8

New technology

The sustainability credentials of the 'Gherkin' in the City of London, designed by Foster + Partners, could only have been achieved with computer modelling and complex construction technology. Aided by the building's curving form, its double-glazed skin creates pressure differentials that keep the interior cool in summer and warm in winter; this passive ventilation massively reduces the need for expensive and environmentally damaging air conditioning.

Foster + Partners, 30 St. Mary Axe ('The Gherkin'), London, 2001–4

Beyond architecture

One of the great opportunities that the sustainability agenda presents for architects is the possibility of widening the debate around architecture to social, political and economic as well as environmental issues. A forerunner in this has been SITE, a New York-based practice led by James Wines (b. 1932), whose holistic, multi-disciplinary approach to design has posed provocative – and playful – questions for the relationship between architecture and the environment.

SITE, Best Products Notch Showroom, Sacramento, California, 1977

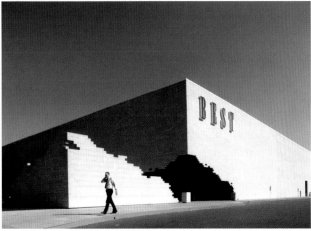

Region: International
Period: 1990s to present
Characteristics: Complexity; Bigness; Cross-programming; Relativity; Seclusion; Iconic

The contradiction inherent in Expressive Rationalism relates to one that defines the work of a wide range of architects from the 1980s to the present day. Advanced capitalism and the shift to service-sector and mass-consumerist economies have created highly fluid, interconnected societies, mirrored in the increasingly multi-faceted complexities of Western, and also Far Eastern, cities. If Modernism sought to express the spirit of the modern age, bringing order and meaning to the chaos unleashed by the Industrial Revolution, Expressive Rationalism constitutes not just its polar opposite but also its complete negation. Revelling in advanced capitalism's absurdities and illogicalities, Expressive Rationalism describes an architecture of fantastically complex, almost surreal forms, achieved with the aid of computer modelling and advanced engineering.

One of the key proponents of the Expressive Rationalist tendency has been the Dutch architect Rem Koolhaas. In his book *Delirious New York* (1978) Koolhaas declared that 'Manhattan is the arena for the terminal stage of western civilization ... a mountain range of evidence without manifesto'. Deliberately provocative on a number of levels – 1970s New York was commonly seen as synonymous with violence and urban decay – what Koolhaas celebrated about New York – its congestion, its incoherence, its fantasy – was a complete subversion of Modernist thinking. Koolhaas regarded the skyscraper – in many ways the ultimate symbol of the inherent irrationality of cities (although perhaps vying with underground railways for that honour) – as the logical consequence of Manhattan's grid system, first laid out at the beginning of the nineteenth century. This archetypal New York symbol, he observed, facilitated new and unpredictable social and economic relations: 'only the Skyscraper offers business the wide-open spaces of a man-made Wild West, a frontier in the sky'.

An important later essay, published in 2001, would see Koolhaas coin the term 'Junkspace' to describe 'what remains after modernization has run its course or, more precisely, what coagulates while modernization is in progress, its fallout'. For Koolhaas 'the built ... product of modernization is not modern architecture but Junkspace, the dismembering of environments, hierarchy, identities and form that was the result of Modernism's fetishization of the singular programme and the means of communicating it. Thus in a number of works by Koolhaas's practice, Office for Metropolitan Architecture (OMA), notably the Seattle Library, the programme is deliberately made complex with seemingly incompatible components operating side-by-side in a relationship that negates straightforward architectural communication. The visual manifestation of this and the broader Expressive Rationalist tendency is radical, highly complex forms, subverting expectations and structural logic, with little, if any, relationship to existing architectural or natural context (which, like Modernist ideology, would in any case be soon superseded and replaced) – all coalescing into a singularity and iconicity intended to evade the banalities of 'Junkspace'.

Complexity

Herzog & de Meuron's 'Bird's Nest' stadium in Beijing crystallizes the inherent contradiction of Expressive Rationalism. Its fantastically complex steelwork appears to evade structural logic in its expressiveness. Yet, with its image beamed around the world during the 2008 Olympic Games, the stadium constitutes a rational response to the need to symbolize China's arrival on the world stage as an advanced industrial power.

Herzog & de Meuron, National Stadium ('Bird's Nest'), Beijing, China, 2003–8

Bigness

In an essay published in his innovative and influential book *S,M,L,XL* (1995), Koolhaas expounded the need for a theory of 'bigness'. Once a building reached a certain size, he argued, normal architectural principles no longer applied; this offered new possibilities for engaging with different urban scales. Thus the curiously scaleless folding façade of OMA's Seattle Library gives no clue to its interior functions.

OMA, Seattle Central Library, Seattle, 1999–2004

Cross-programming

Toyo Ito's Sendai Mediatheque combines a library and an art gallery with a theatre and cafe in fluid, unencumbered dialogue and space. Through the glass façade, its floors appear suspended between twisting, diagrid steel tubes, which as well as providing structural support act as conduits for circulation and services. For its architect, the building was intended to be a microcosm of the city, with multiple programmes co-existing in perpetual flux.

Toyo Ito, Sendai Mediatheque, Sendai, Miyagi, Japan, 1995–2001

213

Relativity

While cross-programming negates Modernism's insistence on the primacy of the singular programme, it also overturns and relativizes existing cultural hierarchies. Luxury goods boutiques and high-end art galleries have increasingly converged and borrow from one another, a prime example being Zaha Hadid's ROCA London Gallery: a bathroom manufacturer's showroom that aspires to be a 'cultural hub'.

Zaha Hadid Architects, ROCA London Gallery, London, 2009–11

Seclusion

Despite Koolhaas's advocacy of, and the infusion of many architects in, the complexities of advanced capitalism, other architects, notably Peter Zumthor (b. 1943), have created works that act to shut out the outside world and instead invite metaphysical reflection. This retreat to an inherently anti-consumerist, somewhat contrived state of authenticity is nonetheless made possible by an architect's fame; Zumthor is able to choose his projects and clients.

Peter Zumthor, Thermal Baths, Vals, Switzerland, 1993–6

Iconic

The way in which Gehry's Guggenheim
Museum, Bilbao, became an instant
icon of the city, heralding much-needed
regeneration, has come to be known as
the 'Bilbao effect'. The iconic building has
proliferated as developers have sought to
exploit the prestige of employing a 'star-
architect' and as planners have acquiesced
on account of the dubious civic (as much
as economic) value of such landmarks.
The soaring, sail-like Burj Al Arab stands
primarily as an international symbol of
Dubai; its function as a luxury hotel is of
secondary importance.

Tom Wright/Atkins, Burj Al Arab hotel,
Dubai, 1994–9

Region: International, especially Europe
Period: 1960s to present
Characteristics: Poetic; Neo-urbanist; Neo-Rationalist; Neo-universalist; Re-interpretation; Layering

By the 1970s Modernist urban planning was under attack from many quarters. The idea of the 'slab in the park' was increasingly unsustainable as architects began to consider how to re-engage with local contexts, traditions and typologies. Among the most sophisticated – and influential – of these was the Italian architect Aldo Rossi (1931–97). His 'Tendenza' movement was inspired by the 1930s Italian Rationalists, notably Giuseppe Terragni (see page 174), hence the coining of 'neo-Rationalist' to describe the work of Rossi and of Georgio Grassi (b. 1935), another of its leading proponents. In his *L'architettura della città* (1966) Rossi set out the movement's theoretical position, establishing a set of fundamental urban types that could be traced back through the work of Le Corbusier, Schinkel, Ledoux and Palladio, as well as Terragni. These recurring types – such as the gate, door, corridor, colonnade or bridge – and their constituent forms – notably the cube, cylinder and cone – could, Rossi argued, be deployed according to present-day needs to create buildings and cities that maintained continuities between past and present; this would avoid the banality of contemporary Functionalism. The sparseness of Rossi's geometrically abstract forms borders on the classical, without reverting to the superficialities of Postmodernism's more literal stylistic references.

Rossi's theories resonated with a number of architects working in the 1960s and 1970s, notably the German Oswald Mathias Ungers (1926–2007). He, along with other neo-Rationalists such as Rob Krier (b. 1938), Grassi and Rossi himself, gained attention for their theories through the International Building Exhibition Berlin (IBA Berlin).

Begun in 1979 under the direction of Josef Paul Kleihues (1933–2004) and completed in 1987, the IBA Berlin sought to find ways of uniting the still-ravaged city under the banner of 'critical reconstruction'. Despite also involving architects whose proclivities differed considerably to those of the neo-Rationalists, the IBA Berlin broadly adapted elements of their typological approach, focusing on the street and the façade, in integrating new buildings with the existing urban fabric.

Underlying Rossi's insistence on recurring types was his contention that the city embodied the collective memory of its inhabitants. For Rossi urban interventions therefore also altered people's collective memory. If those interventions did not conform to the city's pre-existing types, which he argued Modernism was guilty of, then, following his logic, Modernism constituted the actual destruction of memory. Although questionable upon close inspection, Rossi's argument was nevertheless powerful in undermining Modernist thinking and in opening up architecture's frame of reference. The twentieth century was, despite Modernism's ambivalence towards it, generally obsessed with memory – or rather the fear of forgetting – borne out by the proliferation of monuments, museums and archives, not to mention heritage and conservation bodies. Freed from Modernism's constraints, architecture – and thus architects – could now engage with ideas of context and continuity on a much broader level; this opened up new possibilities for imaginative, sensitive or provocative solutions when dealing with both new and historic fabric on the scale of a city or of a single building.

Poetic

The Casa Rotonda, desgined by Mario
Botta (b. 1943), echoes the buildings
of the surrounding Ticino countryside
through its abstracted forms: rectangles
and especially cylinders, added to and
cut away. While clearly inspired by Rossi,
Botta conjures resonances beyond the
straightforward meaning of the building's
forms and context; it encompasses and
exploits the latent tension between the
universal and the local.

Mario Botta, Casa Rotonda, Stabio,
Ticino, Switzerland, 1980–81

Neo-urbanist

While the members of the IBA Berlin sought to reinvigorate the idea of the street, others, notably Léon Krier (b. 1946), went further, arguing for a return to the configurations of traditional European cities after what he saw as the aberration of Modernism. While Krier's critiques of zoning and sub-urbanism had merit, his ideas have lent credence to those advocating a more superficial return to unreconstructed traditional styles.

Quinlan Terry, Richmond Riverside Development, London, 1984–8

Neo-Rationalist

Rossi's neo-Rationalism essentially converged towards a kind of architectural platonism: from an individual city could be derived a set of abstract types and constituent forms irrespective of time period or scale. He sought to reintegrate these forms into an architecture-after-Modernism via various abstract references; the result was sparse, scaleless cityscapes, eerily reminiscent of the work of the Surrealist painter Giorgio de Chirico.

Aldo Rossi, San Cataldo Cemetery, Modena, Italy, begun 1978

Neo-universalist

Siza created the Quinta da Malagueira housing by adapting universal principles to the local context, demographic and topography. The repeating housing units respond to the topography so that each dwelling has an individual identity. Concrete viaducts bring coherence to the whole development, and carry water and other utilities in a conscious echo of the ruined Roman aqueducts nearby.

Álvaro Siza, Quinta da Malagueira housing, Évora, Portugal, 1977–98

Re-interpretation

In his National Museum of Roman Art,
Rafael Moneo (b. 1937) used concrete walls
faced in Roman brick punctuated by arched
openings to create evocative framing
devices, oddly echoing the perspectival
effects of eighteenth-century engravings
by Piranesi (see page 119). Directly
engaging with the museum's historical
subject, the building embodies the idea of
the past reaching us mediated by earlier
generations, and of local history fused
with common Roman heritage.

Rafael Moneo, National Museum of Roman
Art, Mérida, Spain, 1980–86

Layering

Carlo Scarpa (1906–78) was among the
first to integrate overtly modern fabric in
historic buildings; his Querini Stampalia
Foundation, Venice (1961–3), stands as an
allusive analogue of Venice's multi-layered
history. While similar in its layering of old
and new, Scarpa's lyrical approach sits
in contrast to the renovation of Berlin's
Neues Museum by David Chipperfield
(b. 1953), who offered a considered formal
response to a complex and politically
charged project.

David Chipperfield Architects in collaboration
with Julian Harrap, Neues Museum, Berlin,
1997–2009

Postscript

In many ways Heinrich Wölfflin's conception of 'style' and his art-historical method were determined by his subject matter. The flat rectangular façades and proportional systems of the *palazzi*, on which he focused in his seminal *Renaissance und Barock* (1888), lent themselves to the type of formalist analysis he favoured. Today computer modelling allows buildings to be created seemingly in any form imaginable and the use of 3D printing appears to herald a situation in which bespoke components might be fabricated or even designed on-site. In the face of ever-increasing architectural variety, with the very notion of an overriding formal or conceptual framework barely sustainable and architecture's role as an instrument of capital ever expanding, what possibilities are there for 'style'?

Formal groupings according to shared visual characteristics, other than in some vague, essentially subjective sense, are now barely possible and even less useful, given the ease with which a building's form may be manipulated using computer-generated design. Building technologies present a more realistic alternative for categorization yet their commodification and globalization means even new ones soon become part of almost any architect's repertoire. The claims made for Parametricism as an all-encompassing style for post-Fordist society appear simultaneously premature and, following the financial crisis of 2008, now rather dated.

As discussed in the final chapter in this book, the sustainability agenda has the potential to become a new organizing principle for architecture. Demonstrating their apparent proclivity towards totalizing guiding principles, architects have, commendably, been at the vanguard of attempting to modify human behaviour to mitigate the effects of climate change. However, the creation of a sustainable building usually necessitates additional upfront costs, and until such a time that an economic tipping point is reached, architects will almost certainly be fighting an uphill battle. Sustainability in architecture is, of course, a means to an undefined and increasingly debated end. Yet by fundamentally widening architecture's frame of reference, it presents several possibilities in how architecture might develop in the near future.

While the twentieth and twenty-first centuries have seen seemingly exponential increases in building, they have also witnessed unprecedented destruction, not just of the natural environment but of buildings, and even cities. Capitalism's continual process of creative destruction ensures some buildings die so others may be born. Construction is, of course, one of the most environmentally damaging of human activities, and in the buildings and cities that already exist there is colossal embodied energy. Environmental concerns have therefore increasingly turned towards retrofitting and maintaining existing building stocks. Less attention has, however, been accorded to the architectural possibilities this situation presents.

Almost boundless potential exists in augmenting, infilling, adapting, reworking, reconceiving, reconnecting or reinterpreting even the most mundane of existing buildings. New technology and materials can be fused with existing structures and traditional methods, and the whole solution can be tested and modelled thanks to today's freely available massive computer power. Offering the vital combination of constraint, invention and ideology, an approach that might be termed a 'new empiricism' offers architects untold possibilities of creatively engaging with memory, identity and experience, and reconnecting architecture to the fundamental ways in which we shape our built surroundings and, in turn, how they shape us.

Further reading

The date of the most recent or widely-available English-language publication is given here; when different, the original publication date is also given in parentheses.

General
Covering more than one period

Hopkins, O., *Reading Architecture: A Visual Lexicon*, Laurence King, 2012.

Pevsner, N., *An Outline of European Architecture* (1942), Thames & Hudson, 2009.

Summerson, J., *Architecture in Britain, 1530–1830* (1955), Penguin, 1993.

Weston, R., *100 Ideas That Changed Architecture*, Laurence King, 2011.

Wölfflin, H., *Renaissance and Baroque* (1888), Collins, 1964.

Classical

Beard, M. and Henderson, J., *Classical Art: From Greece to Rome*, Oxford University Press, 2001.

Beard, M., *The Parthenon* (2002), Harvard University Press, 2010.

Lawrence, A.W., *Greek Architecture* (1957), Yale University Press, 1996.

Wilson Jones, M., *Principles of Roman Architecture* (2000), Yale University Press, 2003.

Early Christian

Conant, K.J., *Carolingian and Romanesque Architecture, 800–1200* (1959), Yale University Press, 1992.

Krautheimer, R., *Early Christian and Byzantine Architecture* (1965), Yale University Press, 1992.

Gothic and Medieval

Frankl, P., *Gothic Architecture* (1960), Yale University Press, 2001.

Simson, O.G. von, *The Gothic Cathedral* (1956), Princeton University Press, 1998.

Wilson, C., *The Gothic Cathedral: The Architecture of the Great Church* (1990), Thames and Hudson, 2005.

Renaissance and Mannerism

Alberti, L.B., *On the Art of Building in Ten Books* (1454), MIT Press, 1988.

Serlio, S., *The Five Books of Architecture* (1537–75), Dover Publications, 1982.

Vasari, G., *Lives of the Most Excellent Painters, Sculptors and Architects* (1550), Modern Library, 2006.

Vitruvius, *On Architecture* (ca. 30 BCE), Penguin, 2009.

Wittkower, R., *Architectural Principles in the Age of Humanism* (1949), John Wiley & Sons, 1998.

Wölfflin, H., *Classic Art: An Introduction to the Italian Renaissance* (1889), Phaidon, 1994.

Baroque and Rococo

Blunt, A., *Baroque and Rococo Architecture and Decoration*, Elek, 1978.

Downes, K., *English Baroque Architecture*, Zwemmer, 1996.

Hills, H., *Rethinking the Baroque*, Ashgate, 2011.

Neoclassicism

Burke, E., *A Philosophical Enquiry into the Origin of Our Ideas of the Sublime and the Beautiful* (1757), Oxford University Press, 2008.

Campbell, C., *Vitruvius Britannicus: The Classic of Eighteenth-Century British Architecture* (1715), Dover Publications, 2007.

Laugier, M.-A., *An Essay on Architecture* (1753), Hennessey & Ingalls, 1977.

Palladio, A., *The Four Books on Architecture* (1570), MIT Press, 1997.

Semper, G., *The Four Elements of Architecture and Other Writings* (1851), Cambridge University Press, 1989.

Winckelmann, J., *History of the Art of Antiquity* (1764), Getty Research Institute, 2006.

Eclecticism

Howard, E., *Tomorrow: A Peaceful Path to Real Reform* (1898), Routledge, 2004.

Loos, A., *Ornament and Crime* (1908), Ariadne Press, 1988.

Pugin, A.W.N., *Contrasts and The True Principles of Pointed or Christian Architecture* (1836), Spire Books in association with the Pugin Society, 2003.

Ruskin, J., *Selected Writings* (includes excerpts from *The Seven Lamps of Architecture*, 1849, and *The Stones of Venice*, 1853), Oxford University Press, 2009.

Viollet-le-Duc, E.-E., *Discourses on Architecture* (1863–72), Grove Press, 1959.

Wagner, O., *Modern Architecture* (1895), Getty Center for the History of Art and the Humanities, 1988.

Modernism

Banham, R., *Theory and Design in the First Machine Age* (1960), MIT Press, 1980.

Le Corbusier, *Towards an Architecture* (1923), Getty Research Institute, 2007.

Curtis, W., *Modern Architecture Since 1900* (1982), Phaidon, 1996.

Frampton, K., *Modern Architecture: A Critical History* (1980), Thames and Hudson, 2007.

Giedion, S., *Space, Time and Architecture* (1941), Harvard University Press, 2008.

Taut, B., *Alpine Architektur* (1919), Prestel, 2004.

After Modernism

Jencks, C., *The Language of Post-Modern Architecture* (1977), Academy Editions, 1991.

Jacobs, J., *The Death and Life of Great American Cities* (1961), Modern Library, 2011.

Koolhaas, R., *Delirious New York: A Retroactive Manifesto for Manhattan* (1978), Monacelli Press, 1994.

Koolhaas, R., et al., *S,M,L,XL* (1995), Monacelli Press, 1998.

Rossi, A., *The Architecture of the City* (1966), MIT Press, 1982.

Venturi, R., *Complexity and Contradiction in Architecture* (1966), The Museum of Modern Art, 2002.

Venturi, R., Scott Brown, D., and Izenour, S., *Learning from Las Vegas* (1972), MIT Press, 1977.

Glossary

A

Acanthus
A stylized decorative form based on the leaf of an acanthus plant. It is an integral element of Corinthian and Composite capitals, but is also used as a discrete element or as part of a moulded ensemble.

Acroteria
Sculptures – usually urns, palmettes or statues – placed on flat pedestals on top of a pediment. If sculptures are placed at the outer angles of a pediment rather than at the apex, they are called 'acroteria angularia'.

Aedicule
An architectural frame set into a wall, deployed to indicate a shrine in a sacred building, draw attention to a particular work of art or provide additional surface variegation.

Aisle
In a cathedral or church, the space on either side of the nave behind the main arcades.

Altar
The structure or table located in the sanctuary at the east end of a cathedral or church, where Communion takes place. In a Protestant church, a table is usually used instead of a fixed altar for the preparation of the Communion. The high altar is the principal altar of a cathedral or church, located at the east end.

Altarpiece
A painting or sculpture set behind the altar in a cathedral or church.

Ambulatory
The passage behind the altar in a church or cathedral, often linking the chancel aisles.

Apse
The typically semicircular recession from the body of the chancel or, indeed, any part of a cathedral or church.

Arabesque
The term given to intricate decorative mouldings consisting of foliation, scrolls and mythical creatures but omitting human figures. As the term suggests, it derives from Islamic decoration.

Arcade
A repeating series of arches set upon columns or piers. An arcade is termed 'blind' when it is applied to a surface or wall.

Arched brace
In a truss roof, a curved member providing support between vertical and horizontal members.

Architrave
The lowest part of the entablature consisting of a large beam resting directly on the capitals below.

Ashlar
A wall formed from flat-faced oblong blocks of stone laid with very precise joints to create an almost entirely smooth wall surface.

Attic
A room situated just below the roof of a building. In a classical building, it also denotes a storey above the main entablature. On some domes, the attic level is another cylindrical section above the drum, which raises the dome up even higher.

B

Bailey
See Outer ward.

Balconette
A stone balustrade, or most often cast-iron railing, framing the lower section of, usually, an upper-storey window.

Baldacchino
In a cathedral or church, a free-standing ceremonial canopy, usually made of wood and often with cloth hangings.

Ball flower
A roughly spherical ornament composed of a ball inserted into the bowl of a three-petalled flower visible through its trefoiled opening.

Baluster
A typically stone structure, usually set in a row with others to support a railing and form a balustrade.

Balustrade
A series of balusters that support a railing or coping.

Bar tracery
An often quite ornate type of tracery made up of bars: the thin stone rods between the panes of glass that compose the tracery pattern.

Barbican
A further line of defence in front of a castle's gatehouse, often designed to enclose attackers who could then be bombarded from above with missiles.

Barbican also refers to the fortified outposts lying outside the main defences of a city's walls.

Barrel vault
The simplest kind of vault, formed from the extrusion of a single semicircular arch along an axis, creating a semi-cylindrical form.

Base
The lowest part of a column, standing on a pedestal or plinth.

Basement
The storey below the ground storey. In a classical building, the basement sits below the piano nobile at a level equivalent to that of a plinth or pedestal.

Base-structure
The part on which a building sits or from which it appears to emerge.

Basilica
A long oblong building flanked by colonnades (sometimes arcades) that divide the space into a central hall with aisles either side. In ancient Rome basilicas were used for public meetings or as law courts. The building type was adapted for Christian use in the fourth century with many early churches taking this form.

Basket capital
A capital with interlaced carving resembling wickerwork, usually found in Byzantine architecture.

Bas relief
See Relief.

Bastion
In a castle, a structure or tower projecting from a curtain wall to aid defence.

Bay window
A fenestrated projection from a building that may start on the ground floor and extend up one or more storeys. A variation is the bow window, which is curved, while a bay window is typically rectangular.

Blind arch
An arch set into a wall or surface but with no opening. For 'blind arcade' see Arcade.

Brise-soleil
A structure attached to the exterior of a glass-curtain-walled building (though not exclusively so) that serves to provide shade and reduce solar heat gain.

Broken pediment
A pediment whose horizontal base is broken in the centre.

Buttress
A masonry or brick structure providing lateral support to a wall. 'Flying buttresses' are typical in cathedrals and consist of half-arches that help to carry down the thrust of the nave's high vault or roof. An 'angle buttress' is used at corners, usually of towers, and consists of two buttresses set at 90 degrees on the adjoining faces of the two perpendicular walls. When the sides of the buttresses do not meet at the corner they are called 'set back'. A buttress is said to be 'clasping' when two angle buttresses are conjoined into a single buttress enveloping the corner. A 'diagonal buttress' consists of a single buttress set at the corner where two perpendicular walls meet.

C

Campanile
A free-standing bell-tower, usually adjacent to church or cathedral.

Canopy
A horizontal or slightly pitched projection from a building, providing cover from precipitation or sunlight.

Cantilever
A beam, platform, structure or stair supported at only one end.

Capital
The splayed and decorated upper-most part of the column on which the entablature sits.

Capriccio
A type of painting or drawing, popular in the eighteenth century, that depicts works of architecture, often in ruins, arranged in a fictional and often fantastical manner.

Caryatid
A heavily draped sculpted female figure that takes the place of a column or pier in supporting an entablature.

Cella
The central room of a classical temple usually containing a cult statue. The Parthenon, for example, famously contained a long-lost golden statue of Athena.

Cenotaph
A monument commemorating a person or group of people buried elsewhere. Cenotaphs most often commemorate those who have died in war, especially World War I.

Chancel
The eastern arm of a cathedral or church, coming off the crossing containing the altar, sanctuary and often the choir. The chancel is sometimes raised on a higher level than the rest of the cathedral or church and separated from it by a screen or railing.

Chhatri
An open pavilion topped by a dome, a common feature of Indian architecture.

Chevron
A moulding or decorative motif consisting of a repeating pattern of V-shaped forms, often found in medieval architecture.

Chinoiserie
A Western decorative style, popular in the eighteenth century, that drew from Chinese forms, motifs and sometimes techniques.

Choir
The stalled area of a cathedral or church, usually part of the chancel, where the clergy and choir – the group of singers

affiliated to the cathedral or church – reside during services.

Classical orders
An order is the principal component of a classical building, composed of base, shaft, capital and entablature. The five classical orders are the 'Tuscan', 'Doric', 'Ionic', 'Corinthian' and 'Composite', which all vary in size and proportion. The Tuscan, a Roman order, is the plainest and largest. The Doric is found in two distinct varieties: Greek Doric is characterized by its fluted shaft and lack of base; Roman Doric may have a fluted or unfluted shaft and also has a base. The Ionic is Greek in origin, but was used extensively by the Romans; it is distinguished by its voluted capital and often fluted shaft. The Corinthian is characterized by the acanthus leaves decorating its capital. The Composite is a Roman creation that combines the volutes of the Ionic with the acanthus leaves of the Corinthian.

Clerestory
The upper storey of the nave, transepts or choir of a cathedral or church, usually with windows that look out over the aisle roof.

Coffering
The decoration of a surface, typically the underside of a dome, with series of sunken rectangular panels called 'lacunaria'.

Colonnade
A repeating series of columns supporting an entablature.

Column
A typically cylindrical upright shaft or member composed of base, shaft and capital.

Composite order
See Classical orders.

Concave
A surface or form that recedes in the form of a curve. Opposite of convex.

Concentric
A series of shapes of diminishing size but with the same centre, set within one another.

Convex
A surface or form that curves out like the exterior of a circle or sphere. Opposite of concave.

Coping
The typically projecting and often sloped top course of brick or masonry on a balustrade, gable, pediment or wall, which helps to carry off water.

Corbel
A bracket projecting from a wall to support a structure above. When several corbels are combined one on top of another, it is described as 'corbelling'.

Corinthian order
See Classical orders.

Corner pavilion
Structures marking the ends of a range, through featuring a discrete architectural arrangement or through an increase in scale.

Cornice
The highest level in a classical entablature, which projects over the lower levels. The term is also used to refer to a continuous horizontal moulding projecting from the face of a wall, especially where it intersects with the roof face. Or the projecting moulding that tops an aperture surround.

Corrugated
A surface or structure with a series of alternating peaks and troughs.

Crenellations
Regularly spaced 'teeth-like' projections from the top of a wall. The projecting flaps are called 'merlons' and the gaps between are 'crenels'. Derived from defensive structures like castles or city walls, they were later used for decorative purposes.

Crockets
Scroll-like, projecting leaf forms.

Crossing
The name given to the space formed by the intersection of the nave, transept arms and chancel in a church or cathedral.

Cupola
A small dome-like structure, usually circular or octagonal in plan, often placed on top of a dome or larger roof and sometimes used as a viewing platform. Cupolas are invariably heavily glazed to admit light into the space below, and for this reason are sometimes known as 'lanterns'.

Curtain wall
In castles, a fortified wall enclosing a bailey or ward. More generally, a non-load-bearing enclosure or envelope of a building, attached to the structure but standing separate from it. Curtain walls can consist of a variety of materials: brick, masonry, wood, stucco, metal or, most typically in contemporary architecture, glass, which has the benefit of allowing light to penetrate deep into the building.

Cusp
In tracery, a curved triangular indentation in the arch of a curve or foil.

D

Dagger
A dagger-shaped tracery element.

Diagonal rib
A structural rib running diagonally across a rib vault.

Diaper
Any decorative pattern in the form of a repeating grid.

Dome
A usually hemispherical structure whose shape derives from the rotation of a vault 360 degrees through its central axis.

Doric order
See Classical orders.

Drawbridge
A movable bridge which can be raised or lowered over a moat. Drawbridges were usually made of wood and were often operated with a counterweight system.

Drum
The cylindrical, often colonnaded structure on which a dome is raised. Also called a 'tambour'.

Duct
A tube-like structure carrying cables, gases or liquids as part of a building's services.

E

Eave
The part of a roof that overhangs the wall.

Elevator
See Lift.

Entablature
The superstructure above the capital level composed of architrave, frieze and cornice.

Entasis
The convex curve of the shaft of a column that corrects the optical illusion of the appearance of concavity of an entirely straight shaft.

Escalator
A moving staircase formed from a motor-driven chain of steps, usually found inside a building's envelope but also deployed attached to the exterior.

Eye-catcher
A building or structure positioned in a landscape garden to draw the eye and accentuate the beauty of its setting. Typical eye-catchers include temples, bridges or monumental columns; they are almost always follies (buildings with no practical function).

F

Fan vault
A vault formed from many ribs of the same size and curve emanating from the main supports, creating an inverted cone shape with a fan-like pattern. Fan vaults are often highly traceried and sometimes decorated with pendants – elements which appear at the conjunctions of adjacent vaults.

Flat roof
A roof whose pitch is horizontal (though a slight incline is often retained to ensure that water runs off). Tar and gravel are traditionally used to seal the roof, but more recently synthetic membranes are being used.

Flute
A recessed vertical groove on a column shaft.

Flying buttress
See Buttress.

Foil
In tracery, the curved space formed between two cusps, sometimes in a leaf shape.

Forum
A public square in the centre of a Roman town, often used as a marketplace.

Frieze
The central section of the entablature between the architrave and cornice, often decorated in relief. The term is also used to refer to any continuous horizontal band of relief running along a wall.

Frontispiece
A building's principal façade.

G

Gable
The usually triangular part of the wall enclosing the sloping faces of a pitched or gabled roof.

Gallery
In a medieval cathedral, the gallery is an intermediary level standing above the main arcade and below the clerestory, usually set with shallow arches behind which may lie a gallery space above the aisle below. The additional blind arcade that is sometimes present at this level is called the 'triforium'.

Gatehouse
A fortified structure or tower protecting the gateway into a castle. A potential weak point in the castle's defences, the gatehouse was usually heavily fortified and often included a drawbridge and one or more portcullises.

Geodesic dome
A part-spherical or wholly spherical structure composed of a triangulated steel framework.

Gesamtkunstwerk
A German word usually translated as 'a total work of art' and referring to a work of art that brings together many different art forms such as architecture, painting and sculpture. The term was popularized by the German composer Richard Wagner in the middle of the nineteenth century but has retrospectively been applied to many works of the Baroque period.

Giant order (or giant column)
A column that extends through two (or more) storeys.

Glass curtain wall
See Curtain wall.

Grand Tour
A tour of Europe, especially of Italy, undertaken by young aristocratic men (and also artists and architects) mainly during the eighteenth century as part of their cultural education.

Great hall
The ceremonial and administrative centre of a castle, used also for dining and receiving guests and visitors. Halls were richly decorated, often with heraldic ornaments.

Greek cross plan
A church plan composed of a central core surrounded by four transept arms of equal length.

Greek Doric order
See Classical orders.

Green roof
The covering or partial covering of a roof with vegetation (and also including growing media, and irrigation and drainage systems).

Groin vault
A vault produced by the perpendicular intersection of two barrel vaults. The arched edges between the intersecting vaults are called 'groins' and give the vault its name.

Grotesquery
Arabesque-like intricate decorative mouldings that include human figures. The use of grotesquery was inspired by the rediscovery of ancient Roman decorative forms.

H

Hammer beam
In a truss roof, a small beam projecting horizontally from a wall, usually supported by arched braces and carrying a hammer post.

Hammer-beam roof
A truss roof where the tie beams appear to have been cut, leaving smaller hammer beams projecting horizontally from the wall. These are usually supported by arched braces and carry a hammer post.

Hammer post
In a truss roof, a vertical post supported by a hammer beam.

Haunch
The curved part of an arch between the impost and keystone.

Hippodrome
A Greek or Roman stadium for horse or chariot racing.

Horseshoe arch
An arch whose curve is in the form of a horseshoe; it is wider at haunch level than at impost level. Horseshoe arches are emblematic of Islamic architecture.

Hyperbolic parabolic arch
An arch whose curve is formed from the inverted shape of an idealized hanging chain supported at each end.

I

Impost
The typically horizontal band (though it need not be delineated as such) from which the arch springs and on which the springer voussoir rests.

Ionic order
See Classical orders.

J

Jamb
The vertical side of a window surround.

K

Keep or donjon
A large tower at the centre of a castle, sometimes set atop a 'motte' (earth mound), usually enclosed by a ditch. The keep was the most strongly defended part of the castle, where the lord would have resided, and also contained or adjoined the great hall and chapel.

Keystone
The central wedge-shaped block at the top of the arch, locking all the other voussoirs into place.

L

Lancet window
Tall, narrow pointed windows, often grouped in threes; named after their resemblance to lancets.

Lantern
See Cupola.

Lierne vault
A vault with additional ribs that do not emanate from the main supports but are placed between adjacent diagonal and transverse ribs.

Lift
Also known as an elevator, a lift is a vertical transportation device, essentially an enclosed platform that is moved up and down by mechanical means: either by a system of pulleys (a 'traction lift') or hydraulic pistons (a 'hydraulic lift'). Lifts are often in a building's central core but are also found on the exterior.

Light
The opening in a window enclosed by one or more panes of glass.

Lime plaster
Historically, one of the most common plasters, lime plaster is formed from sand, lime and water; animal fibres are sometimes used for additional binding. Lime plaster is used for fresco painting.

Lintel
The supporting horizontal member that surmounts a window or door.

Loggia
A covered space, partially enclosed on one or more sides by an arcade or colonnade. It may form part of a larger building or stand as an independent structure.

M

Machicolations
The holes in the floor between adjacent corbels supporting a crenellated parapet. In fortified buildings machicolations were designed for defence, allowing objects and liquids to be dropped on attackers below, but were later used for decorative purposes.

Mansard roof
A roof with a double slope, the lower slope typically being steeper than the higher one. Mansard roofs often contain dormer windows and are hipped at their ends. A typically French design, the term derives from its first proponent, the French architect François Mansart (1598–1666). If a Mansard roof terminates with a flat gable instead of hips, it is strictly called a 'gambrel roof'.

Medallion
A circular or oval decorative plaque, usually adorned with a sculptural or painted figure or scene.

Metope
The often decorated space between the triglyphs in a Doric frieze.

Mezzanine
A storey sitting between two main ones; in a classical building, the piano nobile and attic.

Moat
A defensive ditch or large trench surrounding a castle for defensive purposes; usually with steep sides and often filled with water.

Mosaic
An abstract pattern or figurative scene created by arranging small pieces of coloured tile, glass or stone – called 'tesserae' – on a surface. The tesserae are fixed into position with mortar or grouting. Mosaics are used as both wall and floor decoration.

Mouchette
A drop-shaped tracery element.

Mullion
A vertical bar or member dividing an aperture.

Muqarnas
A stalactite-like decorative element found in Moorish and other Islamic architectures used to decorate the underside of a high ceiling.

N

Naos
In a classical temple, the central structure of the temple enclosed by the peristasis, usually separated into several compartments.

Narthex
The westernmost part of a cathedral or church, traditionally not always considered part of the church proper.

Nave
The main body of a church or cathedral, extending from the west end to the crossing or, if transepts are absent, to the chancel.

Niche
An arched recess into a wall surface, designed to hold a statue or simply to provide surface variegation.

O

Obelisk
A narrow, tall, roughly rectangular structure tapering upwards with a pyramidal top. Derived from Egyptian architecture, obelisks are used frequently in classical architecture.

Octastyle
A temple front composed of eight columns (or pilasters).

Ogee arch
A pointed arch, each side of which is composed of a lower concave curve intersecting a higher convex one. The centres of the outer two concave curves sit at impost level within the span, or at its centre. The centres of the inner two convex curves stand above the arch rise.

Onion dome
A dome with a bulbous, onion-like shape which terminates in a point at its top; in section, similar to an ogee arch.

Open plan
An interior space with few, if any, dividing walls or partitions.

Orangery
A conservatory or greenhouse-like structure attached to a large house or mansion in the eighteenth and nineteenth centuries, used to grow citrus fruits in colder climes.

Oriel window
A window that projects from one or more upper storeys but does not extend to the ground floor.

Outer ward
Also called a 'bailey'. The fortified enclosure in a castle where the lord's household resided. It also contained stables, workshops and sometimes barracks.

P

Palladian window (also known as a Venetian or Serlian window)
A tripartite aperture composed of an arched central light flanked by two smaller flat-topped windows. Especially grand examples are articulated with an order and ornamental keystone.

Palmette
A decorative motif in the form of a fan-shaped palm leaf, the lobes of which face outwards (unlike an anthemion).

Panel
A rectangular recession or projection in a surface.

Parabolic vault
A vault in the shape of a parabolic curve, most often created using reinforced concrete.

Pediment
A shallow-pitched triangular gable end; a key element of a classical temple front; also often used to top an aperture, not always triangular.

Pendentive
The curved triangular section formed by the intersection of a dome and its supporting arches.

Peripteral
A classical temple surrounded by colonnades on all four sides.

Peristasis
In a classical temple, the single or double row of columns forming an envelope around a temple and providing structural support. Also called 'peristyle'.

Piano nobile
A classical building's principal storey.

Pier
An upright (rarely angled) member providing vertical structural support.

Pilaster
A flattened column that projects slightly from the face of a wall.

Piloti
Piloti are piers or columns that raise a building above ground level, freeing space for circulation or storage in the space underneath.

Pinnacle
An elongated triangular form, narrowing towards the top, extending into the air. Pinnacles are often decorated with crockets.

Pitched or gabled roof
A single-ridged roof with two sloping sides and gables at the two ends. The term 'pitched roof' is sometimes used to refer to any sloping roof.

Plate tracery
A basic type of tracery in which the pattern is seemingly incised into, or cut through, a solid layer of stone.

Plinth
The lowest part of a column base.

Portcullis
A wood or metal latticed gate in the gatehouse or barbican of a castle, which could be quickly raised and lowered by a pulley system.

Portico
A porch extending from the body of a building, usually with a temple front of a colonnade topped by a pediment.

Post
The vertical side of a door surround.

Projecting window
A window protruding from the surface of a wall.

Pronaos
In a classical temple, the porch-like space created at one end of the naos by the extending walls of the cella with a pair of columns placed between the walls.

Pseudodipteral
A classical temple in which the pronaos is articulated by a double row of free-standing columns, the sides and rear having a single colonnade (which may be matched by engaged columns or pilasters on the naos).

Pseudoperipteral
A classical temple whose sides are articulated by engaged columns or pilasters rather than free-standing columns.

Q

Quadripartite vault
A vault in which each bay is subdivided into four parts by two diagonal ribs.

Quoins
The cornerstones of a building. They are often composed of larger rusticated blocks and are sometimes in a different material to the one used in the building.

R

Raffle leaf
A scrolling, serrated leaf-like ornament, often found in Rococo decoration.

Railing
A fence-like structure used to partially enclose a space, platform or stair. The upright members that support the rail itself are often treated decoratively.

Recessed
A feature, say window or balcony, which is set back within the wall surface or building shell.

Rectilinear
A building, façade or window composed only from a series of vertical and horizontal elements.

Relief
A sculpted surface in which the modelled forms project from – or in some examples are recessed into – the surface plane. Bas relief or 'basso-relievo' is a low relief with the sculpted scene extending less than half its depth from the relief plane. In high relief or 'alto-relievo' the scene typically extends more than half its depth from the relief plane. 'Mezzo-relievo' is an intermediate relief between high and low relief. In 'cavo-relievo' the scene recedes, rather than projects, from the relief plane; it is also known as 'intaglio' or 'diaglyph'. 'Rilievo stiacciato' is an extremely flat relief, most often found in Italian Renaissance sculpture.

Render
A form of lime plaster to which cement has been added. Mostly impervious to water, cement plasters are frequently used to render exterior surfaces. Modern cement renders sometimes have acrylic additives to further enhance water resistance and provide colour variation.

Rib
A projecting strip of masonry or brick that provides the structural support to a vault or dome.

Rib vault
Similar to a groin vault except that the groins are replaced by ribs, which provide the structural framework of the vault and support the infilling or web.

Ribbon window
A series of windows of the same height, separated only by mullions which form a continuous horizontal band or ribbon across a building. Ribbon windows sometimes hold concertina frames, which allow the lights to be slid along tracks and folded against one another.

Rise
The height an arch rises from impost level to the underside of the keystone.

Roll
A simple convex moulding, usually semi-circular in section but sometimes more than semicircular. It is usually found in medieval architecture. A variant is 'roll-and-fillet' moulding, which consists of a roll moulding combined with one or two fillets.

Roman Doric order
See Classical orders.

Roof garden or terrace
A paved garden or terrace situated on the roof of a building. As well as providing a place of recreation, especially useful when space at ground level is at a premium, roof gardens help to regulate the temperature in the spaces below.

Rose window
A circular window delineated with often highly complex tracery that gives it the appearance of a multi-petalled rose.

Round-headed window
A window in which the lintel is arched.

Rustication
A style of working masonry in which the joints between adjacent blocks of stone are accentuated. In some forms of rustication, the faces of the stone blocks are further delineated in a variety of ways.

S

Sacristy
A room in a cathedral or church used to store the vestments and other objects used in services. May be within the main body of the building or on the side.

Salon
The principal reception room in a large house that rose in prominence during the eighteenth century as the venue for the exchange of cultural, philosophical and political ideas.

Sanctuary
The part of a chancel where the high altar is situated; the most sacred part of a cathedral or church.

Scroll
A projecting moulding somewhat like a roll moulding but composed from two curves with the upper one projecting further than the lower one.

Segmental pediment
Similar to a triangular pediment except the that triangle shape is replaced by a shallow curve.

Semicircular arch
An arch whose curve has one centre with the rise equal to half the span, giving it the form of a semicircle.

Sexpartite vault
A vault in which each bay is subdivided into six parts by two diagonal ribs and one transverse rib.

Shaft
The long, narrower section of a column between the base and capital.

Sill
The horizontal base of a window surround.

Sliding door
A door set on tracks parallel to the door face. To open, the door is slid along the tracks so that it overlaps with the wall or surface adjacent to the aperture. Sometimes the door slides into the wall.

Solomonic column
A helical column with a twisting shaft. Said to derive from the Temple of Solomon in Jerusalem, Solomonic columns can be topped by any capital. As they are especially ornate, they are rarely used in architecture but more often found in furniture.

Space frame
A three-dimensional truss-like structural framework in which the straight members are arranged in a series of repeating geometrical patterns. Strong but lightweight, space frames are often used to span large distances with few supports.

Span
The total distance an arch crosses without additional support.

Spandrel
The roughly triangular space created between the outer side of an arch's curve, a horizontal bounding above (such as a string course) and the curve of an adjacent arch or some kind of vertical moulding, column or wall.

Spire
A tapering triangular or conical structure often set atop a tower in a church or other medievalized building.

Spolia
The re-use or appropriation of elements from existing or ruined buildings in new ones.

Springer
In an arch the lowest voussoir, situated at the point where the curve of the arch 'springs' from the vertical.

String course
A thin, horizontal moulded banding running across a wall. When a string course is continued over a column, it is called a 'shaft ring'.

Stucco
Traditionally, a hard form of lime plaster used to render the exterior surfaces of buildings, often to hide an underlying

brick structure and provide surface decoration. Modern stuccos are typically forms of cement plaster.

Surround
The general term used to denote the often decorative framing of an aperture.

T

Tesserae
The small pieces of coloured tile, glass or stone used in creating a mosaic.

Tierceron vault
A vault with additional ribs that emanate from the main supports and abut onto the transverse ribs or ridge rib.

Topiary
The cutting of hedges or trees into ornamental forms.

Tower
A narrow, tall structure projecting from the crossing or west end of a church. Also, more generally, a narrow, tall structure projecting from or attached to a building or standing as an independent structure.

Trabeated
A structural system composed from series of vertical posts and horizontal transfer beams.

Tracery
Setting thin bars of stonework between panes of glass, creating an ornamental pattern or figurative scene. See Bar tracery; Plate tracery.

Transepts
In a Latin cross plan (with one arm longer than the other three), the transepts bisect the east end of the nave. In a Greek cross plan, the transepts refer to the four projections from the cathedral's or church's central core.

Transfer beam
A horizontal member intended to transfer loads to vertical supports.

Transom
A horizontal bar or member dividing an aperture, or separating panels in a curtain wall.

Transverse rib
The structural rib running across a rib vault perpendicular to the wall and defining the bays.

Triforium
An additional blind arcade at gallery level in a Gothic cathedral.

Triglyph
A grooved rectangular block in a Doric frieze characterized by its three vertical bars.

Tripartite portal
A large and often elaborate entranceway composed of three openings. Portals are typically found at the west end of medieval cathedrals and churches, and some- times also face the transept arms.

Triumphal arch
An ancient motif of a central archway flanked by two smaller openings. Deployed as a free-standing structure in the classical world, it was revived in the Renaissance and used as a motif on varieties of structures.

Truss
A structural framework of one or more triangular units combined with straight members that can be used to span large distances and support a load, such as a roof. Trusses are most usually constructed from wood or steel beams.

Tunnel vault
Also called a barrel vault, the simplest kind of vault formed from the extrusion of a single semicircular arch along an axis, creating a semicylindrical form.

Turret
Strictly not a spire, but a small tower that projects vertically from the corner wall or roof of a building.

Tuscan order
See Classical orders.

U

Undulating
A building whose shape is composed from intersecting convex and concave curves creating a wave-like form.

V

Viaduct
An elevated bridge-like structure, usually on several arches of small spans, carrying a road or railway across a valley or over a river.

Volute
A scroll in the form of a spiral most often found in Ionic, Corinthian and Composite capitals, but also used in much larger form as an individual element in a façade.

Voussoir
Wedge-shaped blocks, usually of masonry, from which an arch's curve is formed. (Keystones and springers are voussoirs.)

W

Web
The infilled surface between ribs in a rib vault.

Z

Zeitgeist
Originally a German word meaning 'the spirit of the age' and often associated with the idealist philosophy of G.W.F. Hegel.

Index

Picture credits

Acknowledgements

Attempting to chart and distill the history of western architecture into 49 different styles, each with six visual characteristics, is no small task, and one that would have been even harder without the countless other authors who have trodden the ground before me. Their works (many of which are included in the present volume's bibliography) have made this book possible. It is to them that I refer the reader for more rounded accounts – both in detail and argument – than can be included here.

This book is dedicated to Johanna Harding for her loving support and patience during the many months of early mornings and late nights when the book was written.